Justin and Rudy's Tragic Service Desk Project

By

Michael Acton

Edited by Lew Kelsey
Cover Art by T. McCracken

FEEL FREE TO POST COMMENTS ON MY AUTHOR'S PAGE:

amazon.com/author/michaelacton

No part of this book may be copied, reproduced, or transmitted by any means (electronic, mechanical, photocopying, recording or otherwise) without the express consent of the author.

Copyright © Michael C. Acton 2016

Author's note to the reader:

This is the follow-on story to "Justin and Rudy's Excellent IT Adventure." While this book can stand on its own, it does pick up the tale of Justin and Rudy after their success in "IT Adventure." I do weave in the backstory of "IT Adventure" where needed and appropriate to allow the reader to better understand where and how Justin and Rudy came to begin this part of the story, but I do suggest the reader take the time to read "Justin and Rudy's Excellent IT Adventure" to better understand how our IT "superheroes" find themselves in their current state of affairs.

Chapter 1 Part 1

The Start of a New Adventure (Monday May 2nd)

Justin began to wake from the restful sleep he had been enjoying the last few weeks; having remained in a bit of an afterglow as a result of the successful presentation to the company president and board members. As he became more and more conscious, Justin began to realize he was actually in his bed. The thought came as a surprise to him. As a young single man, he was accustomed to falling asleep on the sofa while watching television; ultimately to be awakened the next morning to a televangelist espousing some religious edict or hawking some sort of Bible trinket to the few insomniacs that had the misfortune to be watching at such a Zero Dark Thirty hour. But this was not the case, he began to realize. He was tucked in his own bed in the tiny bedroom of his apartment. The quilt his mother had given him when he moved out on his own was pulled up to his chin, and doing a very nice job of warding off the morning chill that had crept silently and unseen into his bedroom overnight.

As he slowly opened his eyes wider to get a better look at the small alarm clock on the night stand next to his bed, he could see it read 5:27 AM. Much too early for him to get out of bed, he surmised. By now he was much closer to awake than asleep and any attempt on his part to fall asleep again would be nothing more than futile. But he sensed a feeling of utter comfort laying there in the bed and it was more than the feeling brought on by his mother's quilt. He thought back a few weeks when he and his friend, Rudy, "knocked it out of the park" with their presentation to the company CIO, President, and Board Members in their highlights and recommendation of IT Service Management as a way forward in transforming their IT department. Nearly every question asked by the company dignitaries was answered before they finished asking it. It didn't exactly go that way, but that's how Justin chose to remember and recount the briefing to anyone who cared to ask about it. After the presentation, the CIO was practically blushing with pride in what Justin and Rudy had accomplished; and true to his word, there was something extra in their paychecks the following week for a job well done.

He knew better than anyone he wouldn't be able to bask in his company celebrity status much longer as efforts to begin the Service Desk Project were about to begin in earnest. To the CIO, President, and Board Members, this was the single most important edict to come from Justin and Rudy's presentation and all seemed to be on board with it. Most importantly, the funding was already approved. Justin and Rudy would be key players in the build out of this new Service Desk and were justifiably a bit nervous about it. With their recent success, much was expected of them.

Finally, Justin decided a cup of coffee would hit the spot and he began to stir a bit more to toss off the quilt and covers so he could get out of bed.

"You're up pretty early." A strange, yet familiar voice said, piercing the darkness of the bedroom.

Chapter 1 Part 2

Arriving at the office at 5:30 am the CIO of the Southern United Insurance Company, Jackson Jones, wanted to get an early start on this day. He quickly settled in with his coffee and company laptop. He knew the kickoff meeting for the new Service Desk Project was today and although he hadn't purposely avoided preparing for it, with all of his normal duties; it still snuck up on him unexpectedly. Early this morning he decided he wanted to hold his own during the kickoff meeting. The Service Desk discussion with the IT personnel that would attend would certainly understand the concept better than he would, he guessed. Time for an on-line crash course in an IT Service Desk before his day turned crazy; as it always seemed to.

Once his laptop booted up, he began searching sites for a clear and concise description of an IT based Service Desk. He didn't expect to make himself a Service Desk expert in the time he had allotted for the search, and he fully expected interruptions even at this early hour; but he felt he could find enough information on the topic to make himself more comfortable during the kickoff meeting. At the very least, he would have a better idea of what everyone was talking about.

Based on his search criteria, he clicked the most popular return. In a flash the website loaded and he began to scan for useful information on a Service Desk.

The Incident Management process handles all incidents of an organization. Incidents may be failures, questions, or queries submitted by organizational users or technical staff to a service desk, or observed through the use of specialized monitoring software. An incident is defined as an unplanned disruption to an IT service or a reduction in the quality of that service. The primary objective of Incident Management is to resume normal operations as quickly as possible and to minimize the impact on business processes. Incident Management entails much more than simply responding to network outages. A Service Desk is often the function within an IT department that "owns" all incidents for an organization.

Jackson scanned down the page a bit further and continued reading.

An incident is usually elevated by means of a user phone call to the Service Desk, a web user interface ticket created by a user/customer, or from event management software that illustrates an outage of some kind. An incident is not handled until it is known to exist. This is the incident identification step. Next, it must be logged (or registered). This is where a ticket is created in an outage tracking system (such as Remedy or Seibel, for example) to document all relevant information related to the outage. Categorizing the incident is the next step which may highlight what type of incident has occurred. Categories may be based upon the different type of networks or equipment used within the organization. Often how incidents are categorized varies by organization. Priority of the incident must be addressed based on urgency and impact it has on the organization. Priority levels 1 through 4 are often used with 1 being most severe or a major incident. Initial diagnosis occurs when the service desk technician tries to establish what went wrong and how it should be corrected. At this point the technician must determine if the incident can be corrected at their level or whether it must be passed on to a higher skilled technician or engineer for resolution. This is called functional escalation. Depending on the level of business impact, management escalation may also be necessary. Regardless of which entity corrects the problem, the next step is resolution and recovery where a normal operational state returns and the service desk technician resolves or closes the incident record.

Incident Management is a critical component of Service Operation's efforts to maintain the steady state of normal business operations by resolving issues as quickly as possible by virtually any means necessary. However, in most cases during Incident Management the underlying cause of the incident is not directly addressed.

Looking away from the laptop to the window in his office, Jackson noticed it had become a bit brighter outside, but the sun wasn't quite visible yet. He knew that before long people would begin to filter into work and any opportunity to bone up on Service Desk knowledge would be lost. He made a note of the Incident Management and Service Desk relationship so he could mention it during the kick-off meeting.

Jackson looked around his overly large office with décor befitting a company CIO (most of which came with the office and position but was not really to his liking) and once again he thought "I'm in over my head." He came to the CIO position simply by chance and because he had grown tired of his role in Human Resources and saw the CIO position as a challenge and a way to pad his resume. But he had no idea it would be like this; constant calls, usually complaints or requests for new IT services that he only vaguely understood. It wasn't just the company president he needed to keep happy, board members and even branch chiefs wanted changes to the way the IT department operated and the services that were provided. If the Service Desk turned out to be a successful venture, he knew it would reflect well on him as an IT leader and certainly reduce some of the concerns and complaints he heard on a daily basis. Rubbing his eyes before taking a sip from his coffee cup, he clicked the next link in the internet search results; once again with the realization that as the sun rose it wouldn't be long before his phone rang or someone would appear at his door with the first disaster of the day.

Chapter 1 Part 3

When Rudy received his $5,000 bonus for his involvement in the presentation to the company leadership with Justin, he decided to save this windfall for a rainy day. He suspected Justin's bonus was considerably higher than his, but he was content with any sort of bonus. So much so that he never bothered to inquire about Justin's amount. He knew his friend would tell him if he asked, but Rudy wasn't all that interested and was satisfied with his amount and the recognition.

His only indulgence had been early morning visits to the local Starbucks for a tall mocha. He did this every morning around 5 AM; not really because of a craving for a caffeine fix, but mostly because he knew Samantha worked the graveyard shift and until 6 or 7 AM the place would be almost empty of customers. He knew he wanted to spend some time alone with her, even if he wasn't entirely sure why.

Samantha, who actually preferred Samm, the name on her Starbucks nametag, was a slender almost petite young woman in her early 20s. Although she was required to wear her hair tied up in a rather large knot under the obligatory Starbucks ball cap and hair net, Rudy guessed Samm had long, beautiful blonde hair. She was pretty, certainly, but not "movie star" gorgeous. Outgoing, with a better than average smile which she was only too happy to share with customers. What first captured Rudy's attention, then later his heart, were her eyes. They were the most perfect blue. He could only recall seeing the same shade of blue once before in his life. As a young boy his family traveled to the Cayman Islands on vacation. He recalled how beautiful the water appeared as he walked along the beach just outside his family's rented bungalow. It was a "blue" that had stuck in his mind all those years ago and he hadn't seen it again…until the day a few weeks ago when he looked into Samm's eyes for the first time as he ordered his mocha. From that moment on he was hooked.

"Mocha, Rudy?" Samm asked again with that quick mesmerizing smile.

Rudy had just entered the Starbucks and was a bit surprised she was so quick to address him. Then again, he was the only customer at that hour.

"You know me too well." He said as he walked to the counter. "But I think I'll try a white mocha today." As he approached the counter he could see she had already made his mocha and had it waiting for him. She tried to move it to the side, out of his eyesight, but Rudy had already spotted it.

"Is that mocha for me?" He inquired. "That's fine."

"You usually order a plain mocha, so I thought I'd have it ready for you." Samm said, now feeling a bit embarrassed. "Give me a minute and I'll get your white mocha."

Rudy reached across the counter wrapping his hand around the already made mocha…and inadvertently touched Samm's hand in the process.

"This will do just fine…thank you." Rudy said, barely above a whisper, while pulling the coffee toward himself and free of Samm's grasp. Rudy laid his Starbucks Rewards card on the counter and headed to his customary table in the corner.

"Are you sure? It's no trouble to make a white mocha." She said as Rudy turned in the direction of his corner table.

"No, no. I prefer this one." Rudy replied, smiling to himself at the knowledge that she had thought of him and made his drink before he arrived.

Rudy sat down and pulled a book from his backpack, landing with a thud, just as Samm came over to the table to return his rewards card.

"What have you got there, Rudy?" She inquired.

"Oh, we have a big project starting at work today and I needed to bone up on project management…I don't want to look like a complete idiot at our first meeting." Rudy said with a smile.

"You're not an idiot…I think you're nice." She said placing a reassuring hand on his shoulder. "…and I'm sure this project will be great."

Rudy wasn't so sure, but he was glad for the encouraging words and it was reassuring to hear, even if she had no possible understanding of what the project entailed. Actually at this point Rudy didn't either.

"Say, would you like to get a cup of coffee sometime?" Rudy asked without thinking.

For a brief instant Samm looked at Rudy like he had lobsters crawling out of his ears. She spread her arms and looked around the Starbucks and back to Rudy as if to say… "coffee…really? I work in a coffee shop…not the date night I was hoping for."

Realizing his mistake Rudy managed to stammer out "oh, I mean how about dinner?"

"Sure. I would love to." Samm responded with a smile as she handed him a slip of paper. "What's this?" Rudy inquired.

"My cell number."

"Are you in the habit of giving out your number to people?" Rudy asked with a sheepish grin.

"Nope, I wrote it on that piece of paper the first day you came in here…I figured you were going to ask me out eventually…didn't think it would take you this long to ask." She said with a grin, while walking back to the counter just as a few customers began to arrive.

Rudy flipped open the project management book, still with a smile on his face and flutter in his heart.

Chapter 2 Part 1

"Girlfriends all around, Please"

Momentarily stunned to hear a voice from his darkened bedroom as the morning fog began to lift from his brain, Justin started to recall events from the night before. Not waiting for a reply, the voice pierced the bedroom darkness again.

"Did you forget I was here since we kind of tied one on last night?"

Tabitha Carson unexpectedly showed up at Justin's apartment last night under the pretense of discussing the upcoming Service Desk project for which she had been tabbed as the effort's primary stakeholder. Not much was discussed regarding the project before one beer turned into many and ultimately they both ended up in Justin's bedroom. Rudy's comments weeks earlier about Tabitha being Justin's girlfriend turned out to be more truth than the comical fiction Rudy had intended.

"Oh, yes. Good morning. Guess I'm still a bit hung over. Not to mention I'm not used to…you know." Justin started to explain.

"Waking up with a woman in your bed?" Tabitha said finishing Justin's thought. "You have any coffee around here?" she continued the somewhat one-sided conversation while buttoning her blouse as she turned to go back into the bathroom.

"Sure. Just going to put a pot on."

Justin got dressed, feeling a bit embarrassed doing so in front of Tabitha as she watched him in the mirror from the bathroom. Once dressed he tossed her an awkward smile and headed to the small kitchen to get the coffee started.

As beautiful as Tabitha was, combined with the fact Justin didn't have much of a social life, he couldn't help thinking this was a mistake of monumental proportions. For all intents and purposes, she would be his boss on this Service Desk project and he wondered if this new relationship would get in the way. Then again, she was beautiful; and maybe it would all work out. The coffee began to drip into the carafe as she emerged from the bathroom wearing jeans and the white top she wore the night before.

"That coffee smells good." She said as she gathered her things from around the room. One shoe was found hiding under the bed.

"It'll be ready in a few minutes." Justin responded.

"Obviously, I'll have to take mine to go. I need to go back to my place to get dressed for work. The kick-off meeting is today you know."

Justin nodded as he looked for a to-go mug in the cupboard. He located the one and only mug suitable for such a purpose in the back and pulled it out. He held up the mug to show Tabitha like a magician pulling a rabbit out of his hat. All that was missing was the "Ta-da."

"That will do nicely, thank you." Tabitha stated nonchalantly at Justin's display of the one and only travel mug he owned. "Just black will be fine."

She walked over to him and took the mug from his hand. She then placed her free arm around his waist and kissed him…deeply. She smiled as she turned to walk to the door.

"I'll see you at the kick off meeting, sweetie." Tabitha said as she exited the apartment.

Justin stood stunned at his fortune. She seemed really into him and this was completely new territory for Justin. He had never been in any sort of relationship before of any substance…a few dates here and there, but nothing he would have considered sustainable. Regardless of the potential relationship problems that might lie ahead, he smiled as he headed to the bathroom to shave and brush his teeth. Once in the tiny bathroom he reached for his toothbrush…two toothbrushes; a new pink toothbrush had mysteriously materialized…now that's interesting, he thought quickly brushing his teeth. After checking his workplace appearance in the bathroom mirror he headed to Starbucks to meet up with Rudy.

Chapter 2 Part 2

James Walton tapped gently on Jackson Jones' office door fully expecting the company CIO would not be in this early. He opened the door slowly not really expecting anyone to be inside. Mr. Walton was surprised to see the CIO already hard at work at this hour.

"Well, it's nice to see the company CIO hard at work this early." Mr. Walton said as he entered and took a seat facing Jackson's desk.

"I could say the same about you. Why is a company board member walking the empty halls this early?" The CIO replied without looking up from his laptop.

Mr. Walton looked around the office a bit before responding; noting the lack of personal photos and other items in the office.

"I know you haven't been in this position very long, but I figured you would have made this office a little more "yours" by now." Mr. Walton stated.

"Well, guess I've been so busy I just haven't found the time. Is there something I can do for you James?" Jackson said looking up to the company board member.

"You know your IT department is in the crapper, don't you? The board is considering contracting out the entire IT department…have you heard?"

The stunned expression on Jackson's face clearly indicated he had not heard.

"No. I was not aware." Jackson said, his attention now fully invested in what Mr. Walton was saying…the bluntness of the board member's tone came as a shock.

"Look, it's no secret I didn't think you were the right choice for this position. You are a great HR leader, but IT…it's just a different animal. I've always felt, and frankly still do, that we need an experienced CIO running the IT department here. If nobody within the company meets that basic criteria…and clearly no one does…we should look at external candidates. But, everyone else wanted to give you a chance…so here we are with a broken IT department."

"I'm not entirely sure what you mean by broken. It takes time to polish a turd, you know." The CIO said partly trying to lighten the mood that had descended over his office.

"Guess you're right about that." Mr. Walton chuckled. "I'm really curious to see what comes out of Tabitha's kick off meeting today. I'd like to sit in if you have no objections."

"Certainly. Since she was selected by the company president as the primary stakeholder for the project, it's her meeting." Jackson responded. "I would think she would welcome any and all ideas."

"Are your two boys that started this ball rolling going to be there?" Mr. Walton inquired as he got up to leave.

"Justin and Rudy? Of course."

"Look, I know you're doing your best, and I don't mean this as it probably sounds, but just so you know, if there isn't some tangible benefits and improvements from the service desk idea, you might find yourself back in HR. Just my opinion, but there are others on the board and the president, that are warming to the idea of an external hire for the CIO position."

"Thanks for the heads up, I guess." Jackson responded.

"Just thought you'd want to know. Let's hope this project proves successful." Mr. Walton said with a half-smile as he departed.

"Well, shit. This day couldn't start any worse." The CIO whispered under his breath as he slammed the screen down on the laptop. Grabbing his cell phone he walked over to the window and looked out to see the sun finally making its appearance. Swiping down the list of contacts he selected the person he wanted to call. He hit the call button and placed the phone to his ear, while he continued to watch the sun slowly begin to rise over the horizon, ushering in the new day.

Chapter 2 Part 3

Rudy began scanning through his project management book looking for useful information he could use in the Service Desk Kick-off meeting that was now only a few hours away. He knew he couldn't become an expert by simply scanning through a book, but he figured any knowledge he could glean would be to his benefit. Most of what he initially read he quickly dismissed as having no real applicability to the efforts to build the Service Desk. But scanning down through the first chapter of the book something caught his eye that he saw as a potential "project roadmap." Instinctively he knew most experienced project managers would already have an in-depth understanding of these phases…but this was his first exposure and a high level overview was just what he was looking for.

5 Basic Phases of Project Management

Project Management Institute, Inc. (PMI) defines project management as "the application of knowledge, skills, tools and techniques to a broad range of activities in order to meet the requirements of a particular project." The process of directing and controlling a project from start to finish may be further divided into 5 basic phases:

1. Project conception and initiation

An idea for a project will be carefully examined to determine whether or not it benefits the organization. During this phase, a decision making team will identify if the project can realistically be completed.

2. Project definition and planning

A project plan, project charter and/or project scope may be put in writing, outlining the work to be performed. During this phase, a team should prioritize the project, calculate a budget and schedule, and determine what resources are needed.

3. Project launch or execution

Resources' tasks are distributed and teams are informed of responsibilities. This is a good time to bring up important project related information.

4. Project performance and control

Project managers will compare project status and progress to the actual plan, as resources perform the scheduled work. During this phase, project managers may need to adjust schedules or do what is necessary to keep the project on track.

5. Project close

After project tasks are completed and the client has approved the outcome, an evaluation is necessary to highlight project success and/or learn from project history.

Projects and project management processes vary from industry to industry; however, these are more traditional elements of a project. The overarching goal is typically to offer a product, change a process or to solve a problem in order to benefit the organization.

Before Rudy got much further in the book he looked up just in time to see Justin walking into the Starbucks right behind a rather rotund man leading the way. The man went directly to the counter while Justin headed toward Rudy.

"Hey, Good Morning." Justin said, nearly beaming.

"What are you in such a good mood about?"

"Oh, nothing." Justin replied still smiling.

Rudy looked at his friend inquisitively. He knew something was different but just couldn't put his finger on it.

"Look it's nearly time to head to work and you never look this happy when we're about to head to the office. What's going on?"

"Okay, but keep this to yourself…I had an unexpected visitor last night at my apartment."

"You don't mean?"

"I do. She just showed up." Justin explained, in disbelief.

"Tabitha Carson?"

"Yep. You guessed it." Justin responded still beaming with a hint of macho pride.

Rudy kept silent for a few seconds before responding. Trying hard to come up with the best way to tell his friend what he was thinking. He finally just blurted it out.

"Man, this has got disaster written all over it." Rudy said quietly not wanting the other customers to overhear their conversation.

"No kidding…I've been to the movies and office relationships usually end in nothing but trouble." Justin responded, basically rehashing his thoughts from earlier that morning. "Look, she came to my apartment…supposedly to discuss the Service Desk project. And long story short…we woke up the next morning in my bed."

Rudy shook his head, but with a smile on his face essentially realizing the positives and negatives of the situation his friend now found himself in. Rudy had previously kidded Justin about Tabitha; primarily after their successful presentation weeks before when he thought she was giving Justin more attention than was needed. But it was more in jest than anything serious.

"Man, I never thought anything like this would happen. I kind of thought she was "eye-balling" you at the presentation a few weeks ago, but never really thought anything would happen…you know, that she would come to your apartment." Rudy said.

"You and me both. I think she's expecting this to go further."

"What are you going to do?"

Justin thought for a few seconds before responding.

"I guess just roll with it and see what happens." Justin finally responded.

"So, what's the story with the Starbucks girl?" Justin inquired, clearly wanting to divert the conversation to something other than his situation.

Rudy pulled a slip of paper out of his shirt pocket and quickly showed it to Justin. His friend squinted attempting to read the writing on the note, but Rudy tucked it safely back into his pocket before Justin could make out anything.

"So what was that?" Justin exclaimed.

"Her phone number." Rudy responded smiling. "She gave it to me this morning, but she had written her number on the piece of paper the first day I walked in here."

"Guess she had her eye on you, huh?" Justin said.

"Just waiting for me to show an interest as well. I'll call her one of these evenings and set up something with her." Rudy said trying to act as nonchalant as possible.

"Well, I wouldn't wait too long…she might find someone else." Justin half-jokingly responded. "So, what have you got there?" Justin continued, referring to the book sitting in front of Rudy.

"Oh, I was just trying to get some insight out of this project management book before our kick off meeting. Wanted to make sure I had a general idea of what might be discussed if project management terminology gets tossed around."

"Not a bad idea. I'm not sure how this will go or what our roles will be; its Tabitha's meeting so I figured I'd just wait to see what happens." Justin said as he rose to leave. "Guess I'll go into work and check things out...about two hours before the meeting...you coming?" Justin said, glancing at his watch to check the time.

"Not just yet...think I'll read a bit more. I'll see you there." Rudy replied as he once again opened the book in front of him. Justin waved goodbye as he made his way out the door.

Rudy looked over to Samantha and noticed the long line of caffeine addicted customers anxious for their morning fix. He smiled and turned his attention to the book.

Chapter 2 Part 4

Using the Bluetooth connection in her new Toyota Highlander, Tabitha answered the incoming call. She immediately knew it was from the CIO, Jackson Jones. She had hoped to get home from Justin's apartment, get showered and changed before she began getting work calls; but sadly that was not going to happen. She flipped the button on the steering wheel to answer the call.

"Jackson, what's going on?" She answered in as pleasant a tone as possible.

"Tabitha, sorry to call you so early, but wanted to chat with you a bit ahead of the meeting later this morning." Jackson said.

"Sure, should I come by your office later?" She said as she pulled into her driveway; thinking that it really wasn't that early anymore.

"That would be great. I just want to get an idea of where you think we are with the Service Desk Project ahead of the Kick off Meeting."

"I tell you what, I'll send you my slides and you can look them over prior to my arrival. How does that sound?" She said reassuringly; as she could hear the nervousness in Jackson's voice.

"Sounds like a plan…thanks." He responded before clicking off the call feeling a bit odd asking for help with something he should already have a solid understanding about.

Jackson returned to his desk and sat down in front of his laptop and hit refresh…15 new emails popped in.

"Great." He said sarcastically as he slammed his laptop closed for the second time this morning.

Chapter 2 Part 5

Rudy knew that he wanted to know more about the stakeholder role in a typical project, yet he fully expected this Service Desk project to be anything but typical. He thought that most projects; based on what he'd read and heard about project management, turned out to be anything but typical. Was there even such a thing as a typical project, he thought. Flipping through the book he found a short chapter titled, "Handling Stakeholders and their Role in Project Success." He scanned through and read the following section of the chapter.

If you think about it, you often have no control over key stakeholders: for example, regulatory agencies, customers, and your sponsor. Therefore, you want to focus on understanding their needs and the relationship to the project:

- *Know that each stakeholder may have specific requirements.*

- *Do the stakeholders support your efforts regarding the project?*
- *What impact will your project have for each stakeholder?*
- *How should you communicate with them?*

Consider these approaches when managing project stakeholders:

- *For those stakeholders with a high degree of influence, you need to plan how to maximize their positive influence and behavior. In other words, you want to deliberately figure out how to optimize their engagement level and their engagement type with your project. Leverage powerful stakeholders who support your project by asking them to champion the project to others, especially those who are more resistant to the project.*
- *For powerful stakeholders who are not supportive of your project, you want to find a way to minimize the potential for them to disrupt the project or slow progress. You might do this by finding even a little benefit for them, or you might appeal to their sense of loyalty to the organization.*

Sometimes, the best you can hope for is that the stakeholders who don't support your project will remain in the back ground and not be disruptive.

Throughout your project, you should stay in communication with key stakeholders and check in to see whether their support level has changed. You will also want to see whether your engagement strategy is effective. You may need to revisit your approach to managing their engagement if your initial plan was not successful.

Just reading this short section concerned Rudy, because he knew there would be conflicting priorities between various stakeholders. The IT department leads (Servers/Networks/DSS/Phones) likely wouldn't want anything to do with the Service Desk and even if they all agreed that the effort was needed, there would certainly be disagreements on implementation and the role it plays. He knew from past experience that breaking down company silos would be a challenge because change is usually not well received by most.

The IT teams were comfortable in their current state; and there would be resistance to anything meant to alter that; regardless whether there were direct benefits to such a change. He realized that if this project was going to succeed, it would largely fall on the shoulders of Tabitha as the Project Manager and Primary Project Stakeholder…then he thought it odd that she was both for the same project. Wasn't that a conflict? If the PM's role is to drive the project to conclusion, shouldn't that person be somewhat neutral so all stakeholders can be equally heard? Otherwise, Tabitha may just steer the project to meet her perceived expectations omitting the concerns of other, just as important stakeholders.

Other concerns swirled around in his mind as he looked around the Starbucks and noticed the place had quickly transformed from his early morning library into…well, a crowded Starbucks. He realized he wouldn't be able to concentrate on the book any longer, so he might just as well head off to work. Getting up to leave, he shot a smile in Samm's direction and she returned it with the "Call me" gesture of thumb and pinky finger held up to her ear and mouth while at the same time silently says the words,

"Call me."

Although concerned about the project as he departed the coffee shop, he was smiling as he headed to his car. In fact, the same smile would be painted on his face all the way to work.

Chapter 3 Part 1

"Kick-Off Meeting: Who Exactly is Driving this Train?"

Jackson Jones finally saw the email arrive from Tabitha and he quickly opened it. It read: *Jackson, see the attached PowerPoint presentation. I'll be at your office shortly and we can discuss any questions or concerns that you might have. I plan to conduct the brief to the team, but I want you to feel free to chime in as appropriate. This will need to be a team effort if we are to succeed...obviously☺ See you soon. T.*

Jackson clicked the email attachment and began to scan through the slides. Initially, he found the brief to be the typical format used at Southern United Insurance Company and thought it was rather unremarkable for something with such high visibility. But, as he began to read each slide in detail, he began to see that all the pertinent data he expected to find within the briefing was present. He did wonder about a couple of things he noticed on the second to last slide within the deck...why was Tabitha's name in larger font than the rest of the Key Project Players on the slide and where were the other key players from non-IT departments of the company?

Jackson didn't really care if Tabitha felt she was the most important person on the project and wanted to make that known by ensuring her name was first and foremost on the slide; he just thought it a bit odd that anyone would do that to make a point…whatever point that happened to be, he wasn't quite sure. What he did find a bit disturbing was the clear absence of other non-IT key players within the company that would certainly need to be aware of the Service Desk project; even if they didn't have much input to provide…claims processing department for one. He jotted down a note to bring that up during the meeting.

Having some insight into what the meeting would now entail, he felt better about his level of understanding of the project; although he wasn't to the point where he felt very comfortable and could lead such a discussion, he did figure he could muddle through now without appearing to be the village idiot of the IT Department. That would have to be enough. Jackson now began to review the other unopened emails in his queue; in part to see what other fires required his attention, but largely to kill time until the meeting.

Chapter 3 Part 2

Rudy arrived at work later than normal and was surprised to see an abundance of available parking close to the building. He chose a corner spot next to a small tree with the thought that it would at least provide some relief from a door ding to one side of his vehicle; yet likely result in bird poop from nesting birds in the tree. He concluded the poop could be washed away, while the door dings were more permanent and becoming a constant source of employee concern due to the extremely narrow parking spaces. There had been efforts to get the lines in the parking lot redrawn a few years ago when an employee drawdown had resulted in fewer cars needing parking. Some employees would simply park using two spots; however Rudy was reluctant to do the same. As Rudy exited his car, he glanced up at the tree and for the time being saw no bird bombers in sight; though he knew that wouldn't last long.

Walking toward the building he saw Justin sitting in his car a few rows closer than he had parked. He approached the driver's side window and tapped on the window. The sound initially startled Justin, as he was listening to his CD player and reading the back of the CD case.

"What are you doing?" Rudy inquired.

"Listening to this book on CD…it's pretty good." Justin responded.

"Why are you out here?"

"Man, its dead in there this morning. I was just getting ready to go in and head to the conference room. There are no jobs right now…I checked not 10 minutes ago."

"I'll walk in with you." Rudy motioned to his friend.

"Hey how about a coffee on the way up to the conference room?" Justin inquired.

"Sure, if you're buying."

"Man, you're like a broken record." Justin said smiling at Rudy's remark; as it seemed Justin was always on the hook to purchase his friend's java.

Justin didn't mind, in fact, he was glad to do it. Rudy was a good friend and he had really stepped up in putting the initial presentation together and had conquered some of his fears in the process. Justin was very proud of Rudy for that. Rudy has never been very social and to speak in front of company dignitaries was a major challenge; but he did a great job and Justin was proud of his friend for the strides he'd made since that stressful day. Once inside the building both made an abrupt right turn and headed in the direction of the cafeteria.

Although past the usual time for the morning breakfast rush or the early morning coffee addicts, there were more than a few stragglers inside the cafeteria; chatting about their weekend events or simply not in a hurry to get back to work because they had little to do or just didn't want to do it. The meeting was scheduled for 10 AM and by the time they got coffee; which Justin again paid for, it was 20 minutes of ten, so they headed straight for the conference room to get a couple of prime seats. Not knowing how many or who would be in attendance, they thought it best not to walk in at the last minute; especially since both were tabbed as key players on this project…it would not send a good signal to others asked to join the effort.

Stepping off the elevator on the CIO floor and walking down the hall, they spotted Mrs. Evans sitting in her customary spot in her cubicle outside of the CIO Conference Room. As they approached both experienced a vague feeling of déjà vu from the only other time they attended a meeting in that conference room. On that occasion, the presentation to the Board of Directors and President had been a rousing success. There was no reason to think this meeting wouldn't be likewise. After all, once you've been to the mountaintop, shouldn't the second ascent be easier?

"Everyone has arrived except Ms Carson. You two should better get in there." Mrs. Evans stated without so much as a casual glance in their direction. She just continued typing on her keyboard.

Justin and Rudy looked at each other, surprised they were nearly the last to arrive, as they entered the conference room.

Chapter 3 Part 3

Once inside they quickly looked for a place to sit and were initially shocked at the number of people sitting patiently waiting for the meeting to begin. Steve Parker, the Desk Side Support (DSS) supervisor, who also happened to be their boss, waved them over to a couple of seats at the table where he was sitting.

Steve obviously had saved these seats for his two subordinates. "Glad you could make it." Steve said in a joking manner, and with a voice soft enough that only they could hear.

"Surprised so many got here this early." Justin replied.

Folks were murmuring in low tones throughout the room, mainly just chit chat and nothing related to the briefing about to start. Justin and Rudy quickly scanned the room to see who was in attendance. There was a beautiful young woman dressed in her best workplace attire sitting with a memo pad ready to go; clearly there to take notes of the meeting. She was likely someone's administrative assistant. Neither Justin nor Rudy knew who she was. There was a young man in the back of the room sitting in front of a computer, there to present the slides of the briefing. With that Justin and Rudy finally noticed the first slide of the presentation prominently displayed on the screen at the front of the conference room.

The CIO Jackson Jones was toward the front of the room "playing" with his company issued cell phone and sitting next to him was James Walton one of the company's board members who had participated in the briefing Justin and Rudy presented a few weeks ago. Paul Simmons, the Voice Shop supervisor was there; looking like he preferred to be anywhere else. Becky Wisdom and Marcus Hollister; the server and network leads respectfully, were at the table also wishing they could find a way out of this meeting…based on the "sour puss" looks on their faces…although to be fair, Becky usually looked that way. She had short cropped hair and was a little thick in the middle, but as a former Marine, she was not someone to mess with. Marcus was young for a supervisor and although quiet and unassuming, more times than not he did as his leadership asked of him. Jackson seemed to be a bit agitated as he clearly wanted to get the meeting started. With that, Mrs. Evans popped her head in and announced to the group that Tabitha was in the building and would be up shortly.

"It's about time." James Walton exclaimed to mock chuckles from the group. But as it turned out, Tabitha wasn't that late…everyone had just arrived earlier than they needed to; which gave the false sense that anyone arriving later was overly late; which technically wasn't the case. Only a couple of minutes passed before Tabitha Carson strode into the conference room.

She looked nothing like she had earlier that morning at Justin's. She wore a dark red skirt with matching blazer with a white blouse. Her pumps were also red, matching the rest of the attire; heels moderate height befitting the business attire and her status as a professional woman. Her hair was neatly tied back without a strand out of place…make up was conservative, noticeable and perfectly applied.

"I'm so sorry to be late." She said as she entered the room, briefcase in hand and headed straight to the lectern in the left front corner next to the projected image on the screen. Wasting no time she opened her briefcase, retrieved some papers, then quickly closed and set the case to the side, out of the way. "I assume you all know why we're here today and everyone should know each other…However, for those of you who may not know, this is Chyna. I've asked her to take notes of today's meeting." Tabitha said, pointing to the beautiful young woman with the memo pad.

Chyna flashed a small wave and a thousand dollar smile to no one in particular and proceeded to flip open the memo pad. It seemed to Justin that Becky took more than a casual chance to acknowledge Chyna as she was the only one in the room to wave back. Chyna didn't seem to notice or care, but Becky's "sour puss" expression disappeared for a short time. A lesbian thought rose in Justin's mind, but he quickly dismissed it. Justin refocused as Tabitha began.

"First I would like to thank James Walton, one of my closest friends on the board for attending today. Your insight and assistance has been a godsend." She began.

Friend? What the hell did she mean by that? Justin thought, feeling a pang of jealousy creep up from nowhere.

"Also, I would like to thank Jackson for all his support in getting this project moving in the right direction." She said pointing to the CIO. "With that lets' get started."

Rudy leaded over Justin and whispered, "No intro for us? Didn't we start this train down the tracks?"

"Shhhhh." Justin replied quietly.

"For those of you who may not know me, I'm Tabitha Carson and a member of the board. I've been on the board for a couple of years now. Previously I was the Senior VP for Infrastructure Development for an IT company in the Midwest. I have a Master's Degree in Business Administration from Stanford University and I'm thrilled to be a part of this company. When President Ferguson asked me to take the lead on this effort, I was thrilled. I see real benefits to the creation of the Service Desk concept…primarily cost and resource savings. So, Buster, let's get started." She said motioning to the young man behind the computer in the back of the room.

Justin and Rudy would later learn his name was, in fact, "Buster" and much like Chyna he was an administrative assistant from some big wig from the Claims Department borrowed to assist with the briefing.

With that queue from Tabitha, Buster advanced the briefing to the next slide in the deck.

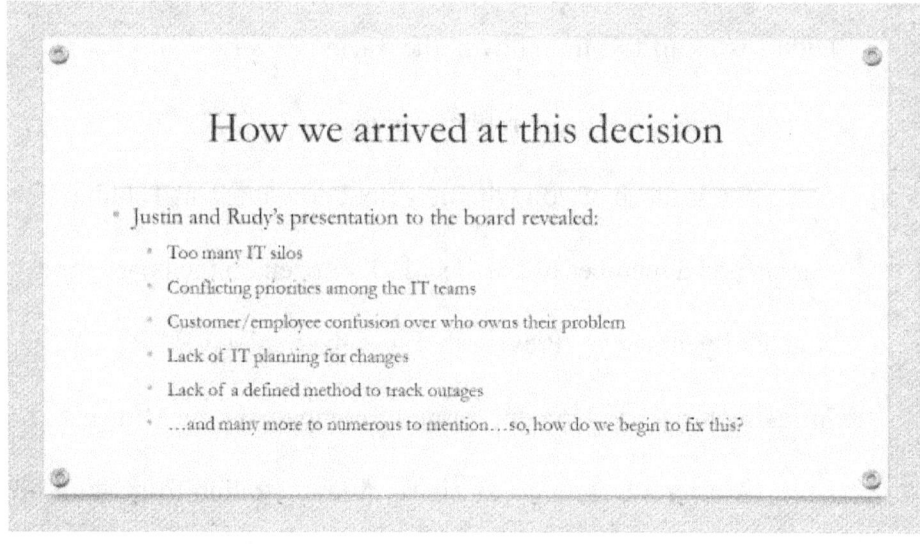

"You may be asking yourselves why we're doing this now." Tabitha continued as the new slide appeared at the front of the conference room. She glanced over to the screen to verify that the proper slide was displayed.

"Let me explain how the company and its leadership came to this decision. A few weeks ago Mr. Jones asked Justin to investigate the feasibility of implementing some aspects of IT Service Management into our day to day IT processes. Justin in turn enlisted the help of Rudy and both embarked on a journey of discovery within the IT department and frankly discovered things that we could improve upon. As you can see on the slide we have too many silos within the IT department and conflicting priorities among the IT sections."

"Just a second…I'd like to say something here." Becky shot up; providing the first dissenting voice in the meeting.

"You have a comment?"

"I don't see the problem with a silo structure and why would anyone really care what my team's priorities are?" Becky chimed in. Without skipping a beat, Tabitha shot back.

"Have you ever experienced a situation where Marcus' team did something that affected your mission?" Tabitha inquired, knowing the answer already.

"Well, yeah. Just last week I found out after the fact that they pushed a patch or something that took down one of our servers." Becky responded pointing blame toward the network team.

"Okay. Had you known this action by Marcus' team was about to take place, what would you have done? Probably moved the Primary server over to a secondary, right?" Tabitha inquired.

"I suppose so." Becky said, realizing her argument was about to lose any viable traction.

"I would hope so. If you were aware of a change happening that was going to take down one of your servers, I would hope your team or any other team would take the necessary actions to prevent service loss. In your team's case putting the secondary server on line while the network action was taking place would have made this change action by the network team seamless to the users of those services and applications housed on that particular server." Tabitha concluded.

She is brilliant. Justin thought.

Clearly Becky had resigned herself to not push the topic any further…however the "sour puss" expression had returned.

"Any other questions or concerns about where or how we arrived at this decision? Before I forget, I'd like to thank Justin and Rudy for their efforts in getting us to this point. Great job guys. Next slide." Tabitha said to a smattering of applause for Justin and Rudy.

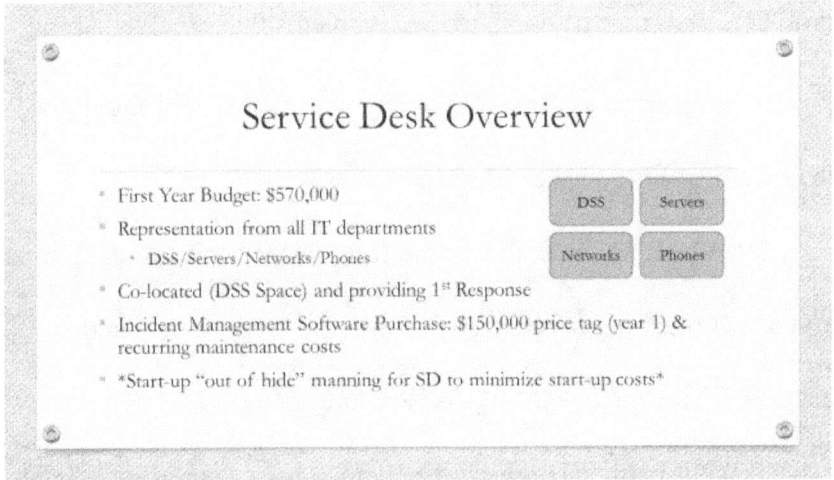

"The good news is that we have an approved budget for the Service Desk for the first year. Leadership will reevaluate future funding based on success achieved the first year...meaning faster outage resolution times for customer outages, less self-inflicted wounds as Becky just highlighted IRT to teams doing work unknown by the other teams...things of this nature." Tabitha begun.

"Most of these metrics that will illustrate the viability of the Service Desk will come from data from the Incident

Management software, right Tabitha?" Jackson interjected.

"You are right, Jackson. This software will allow us to track outages, length of time it takes to fix something, types of problems that must be escalated vs. problems that are fixed at the lowest level…and a myriad of other metrics that will highlight the benefits of the service desk."

"Where do the bodies come from to staff this thing? I hope you aren't planning to snag any of my guys. I'm short-handed already." The voice team supervisor, Paul inquired.

"Well, that's what the last bullet means…"out of hide." Tabitha responded.

"Paul, look at it this way. You are really not losing personnel on your team. The person from your team that is assigned to the Service Desk will be working many of the simpler issues so the rest of your team can concentrate on the more complicated voice outages and issues. It's a more efficient use of your resources." Justin chimed in ahead of Tabitha's response.

"Exactly. I think this will work out better for your teams in the long run." Tabitha concluded.

Marcus, the network lead spoke up.

"Oh, I get it. So the easy stuff like just bumping a network interface, which happens frequently, would be done by the network guy working the service desk. It would never even get to our network shop; which in turn frees us to do other things."

"Exactly right." Justin said.

"There is one thing you forgot. What if no one wants to work the service desk?" Becky inquired.

"If they want to continue to work here, they need to be team players and do what we ask. This is the direction I want you leaders to take back to your teams." Jackson chimed in, speaking like a true CIO. "Since our service desk will handle the more routine problems, you probably want your service desk representatives to be some of the lesser experienced technicians."

"That's right Jackson." Tabitha said. "Are there any other questions regarding this slide? Okay let's move on."

Where do we start?

- Some tasks already under way…Cube space allotted; cabling underway.
- Begin with a Plan…Tabitha working on it
- Project Lifecycle---Plan / Do / Evaluate / Repeat
- Project Scope – Don't over or under reach. Deliver what is promised.
- Manage the project to completion.

"The positive takeaway here is that we are not starting from square one. As you can see from this slide, we've already begun some activities." Tabitha stated.

She explained the service desk cubicles were already set up and the cabling for all four cubes where the service techs would sit has been underway and nearing completion. She went on to explain about the goals of the project and the project plan which few really understood, except Rudy and Jackson. Rudy had been reading the project management book a little so he at least understood the terminology she was using. Jackson, on the other hand, had been involved in other projects when he worked in the HR department prior to coming to his position as the company CIO. She stressed extensively the importance of staying within the scope of the project and not fall victim to scope creep as that would certainly result in a budget increase the company and team couldn't afford. Little comment was exchanged regarding this slide as everyone assumed Tabitha had control over managing the project from start to finish and everyone else would simply carry out project tasks at her direction. With that she motioned to advance to the next slide.

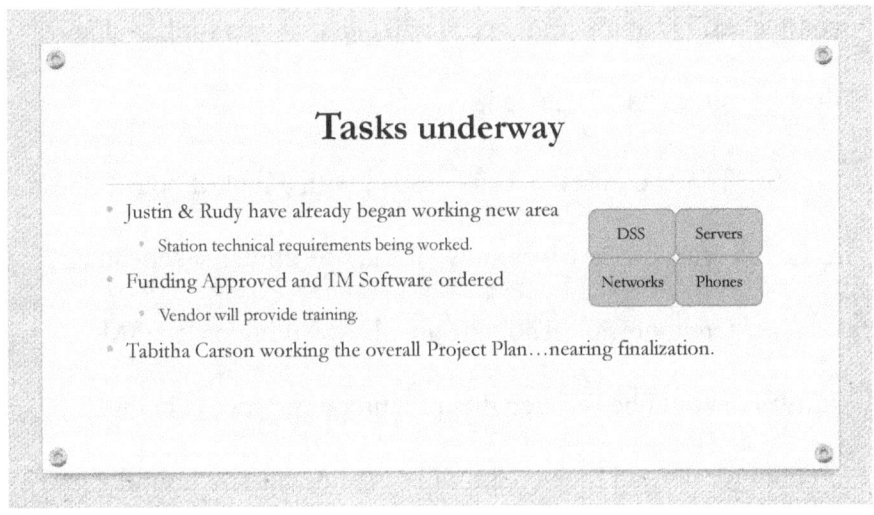

"Guys..." Tabitha stated while casting her gaze in the direction of Justin and Rudy. "...why don't you explain a bit to the group exactly where we are in the current build out of the Service Desk spaces."

Rudy was the first to speak up.

"Well, as Tabitha mentioned earlier Justin and I have nearly completed the set-up of the spaces the new Service Desk techs will occupy. Really all that is needed is to ensure access to specialized functions and applications are available and work for each tech. Like for instance, test phone and call manager access for the voice tech work space."

"So, cabling and baseline workstation configs is completed?" Tabitha inquired, realizing this was further along than her slides had indicated.

"That's correct." Rudy replied with a hint of boastfulness, as he too realized they were now ahead of Tabitha's schedule.

"Great news." Tabitha agreed. "Moving on, the IM software should be through the procurement process in the coming weeks and the vendor will schedule on-site training shortly thereafter. Additionally, although we have clearly begun and apparently completed some of the project tasks, it's just as critical to have an overall project plan with each plan task clearly outlined and scheduled based upon the overall project timeline...along with dependencies for each tasking."

Only Jackson and Rudy really understood what she was talking about. Then again, the remainder of the group didn't figure it was important they understood basic project management concepts. They assumed tasks would be handed out and they would complete them as directed by Tabitha.

"So, within the next couple of days, I'll have the overall plan sent out to everyone so you can review it. We'll meet again to discuss each project task and timeline one by one, okay?" Tabitha commented, indicating to Buster to advance to the next slide.

"We've already talked about some of the high level tasks that need to get done. This slide just reiterates some of those tasks. Again, a more detailed plan will be provided to all of you in just a few days." She explained. "The big take away from this slide is what Jackson alluded to earlier. You IT section leads will need to start thinking about who from your team will be assigned to the Service Desk...at least initially. We can discuss later, but there may be some benefit in making these assignments rotational. It's just a concept to think about as we move forward."

Tabitha gave the group a few minutes to digest this slide. When she realized there were no questions or comments coming, she moved on to the next slide.

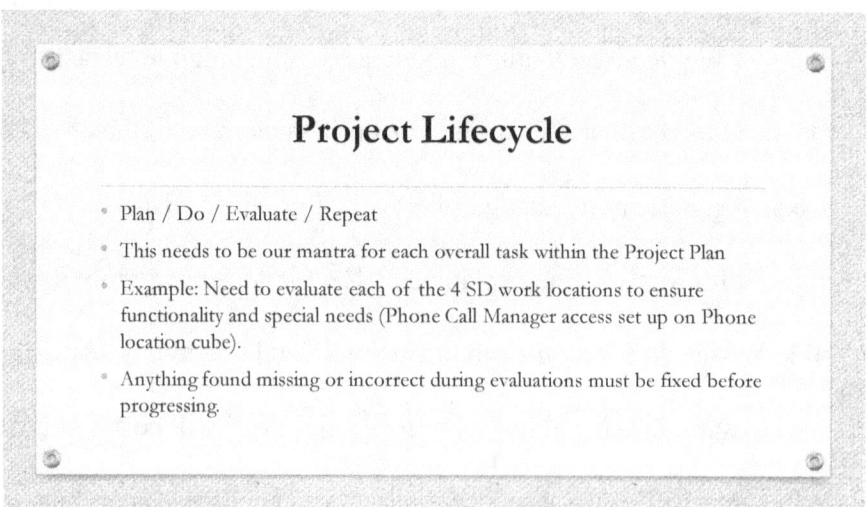

Tabitha spent about ten minutes discussing this slide giving a high level overview of the lifecycle of projects spending more time discussing the "evaluate" part than the others. In her view this was most critical as she emphasized, each critical step in the project must be evaluated to ensure it passes muster. If a particular task is simply implemented without being adequately tested, it would jeopardize the entire project's success. If errors were found later in the project due to a lack of adequate task testing, it could cause a significant amount of re-work and project delay; not to mention added expense which the company couldn't afford.

"No cutting corners here people." James Walton chimed in, speaking for the first time during the briefing; having been engaged with his cell phone during much of the meeting to this point.

"Right James." Tabitha stated. "Let's do it right the first time and verify that it IS right." On cue, the next slide appeared.

Project Scope

- Deliver what is promised...nothing more and nothing less
- The board send out a Project Scope document a couple of weeks ago, so we should all know what is in scope.
- Any deviations to the scope need approval from Tabatha Carson.
- For example: a request for a more powerful computing platform mid-project is scope creep as requirements are already known.

"I'm not a PM, so I'm a little fuzzy on Scope." Marcus interjected before Tabitha could start speaking to this slide.

"No worries there. There are a host of real project managers that fall victim to allowing their projects to fall out of scope. The idea here is to deliver the requirement. Nothing more and nothing less. What often happens in projects is there is an unidentified or uninvolved stakeholder which comes into play later in the project lifecycle with a new or modified requirement. If we simply accommodate this change without it being fully vetted, the overall scope of the project could change or expand beyond what the resources and project can withstand. This is referred to as scope creep. As the slide mentions, you all should have received a copy of the scope document last week. If you haven't read it, I encourage you to do so. If you have any questions please let me or Jackson know ASAP. Any questions before we move on to the next slide?" Tabitha concluded pointing to the slide.

"Just a minute, please." Becky chimed in before the next slide was displayed.

"Yes?" Tabitha responded.

"Based on your slide there, if someone…someone important, I guess, comes to us mid- task and requests some change or modification to the existing task we're working we should contact you for guidance before proceeding, correct?" Becky inquired.

"That's right."

"Well, what if you aren't around. I mean, what if we can't reach you for a decision? Should we just delay the project until you're available?" Becky inquired, knowing she was backing Tabitha into a bit of a corner.

"I assure you that I'm as committed to this effort as anyone and will be available to support this project 24/7." Tabitha shot back.

"I'm sure you are, but sometimes the unforeseen happens and it seems to me that it would be prudent to have a back-up to make project decisions."

"If anything were to happen to me, I'm sure Jackson is more than capable of making project decisions in my absence." Tabitha stated putting an end to Becky's concerns. "May we move on now?"

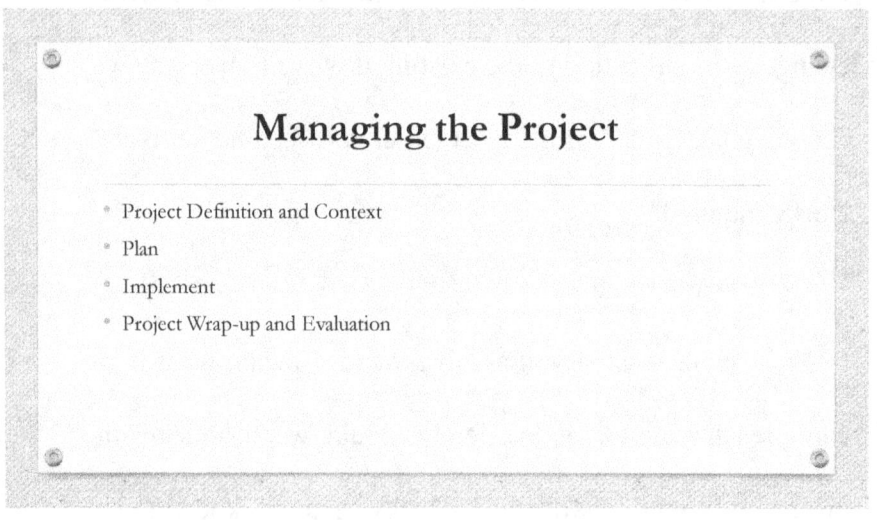

Having been taken out of her game a bit by Becky's questioning of her "one belly button project decision maker" philosophy, Tabitha breezed through the "managing the project" slide faster than she intended and immediately called for the next slide forgoing the option for questions from the group.

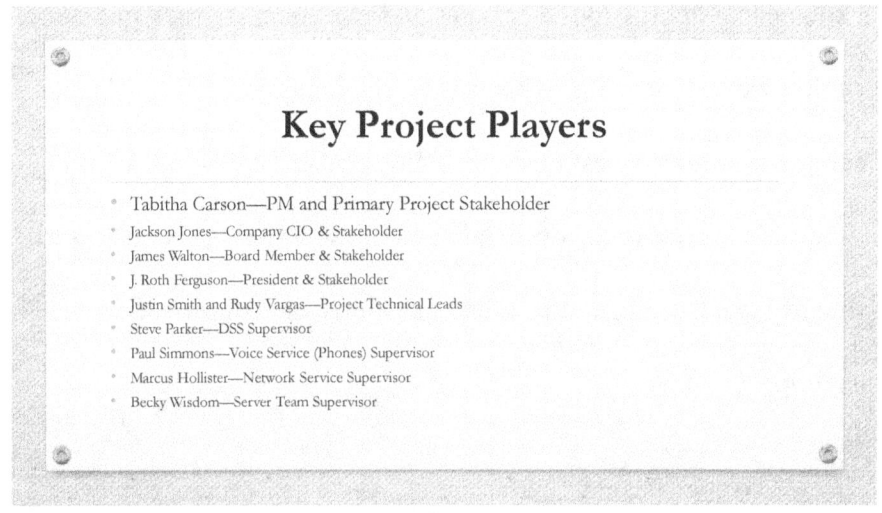

"The point I'd like to make here is that the company leadership and board of directors see each of you as integral to this project's success. This means the work your teams need to perform will be your responsibility to ensure it gets completed and within the scope of the project and on schedule. This isn't to say that you must do the work yourself, but you are expected to manage the work and report task completion so if another task by another team is dependent on the completion of your task…they will know they can proceed with their work. Make sense?" Tabitha stated, back on her game now.

She motioned to move to what was the final slide, egger to

get to any final thoughts or questions the team had. As the final slide came up, she took her notes and placed them back into her briefcase and closed it. This was a time honored subliminal tactic to avoid further questions where the speaker begins to pack up their notes prior to the "official" end of the briefing, but it was to no avail as there would be a few questions and concerns from the group.

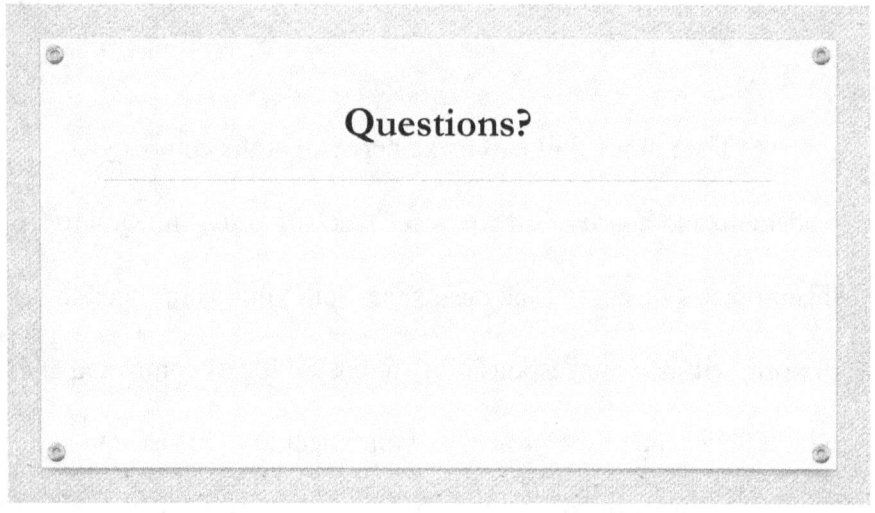

"Is there a timeframe for completing this project?" Marcus inquired.

"Yes. Roughly six months, but we'd like this done sooner so we can show real benefits to leadership." Tabitha announced.

Marcus nodded his head in agreement.

"Will everyone receive this training or will it just be for those working on the service desk?" Paul inquired.

"Good question. Since tickets will be created at the service desk and routed to the individual IT departments when necessary, it's important that everyone receive this training. The vendor has agreed to train as many folks as we need." Tabitha responded.

There were a few other questions asked as the group began to mingle toward the door to depart. None seemed particularly important, so Justin and Rudy began moving in that direction as well, although Justin really wanted to say something to Tabitha regarding how well she did, but thought better of it. Just as they got to the door to leave Jackson Jones called out to the boys and asked them to say behind for a few minutes.

Chapter 4 Part 1

"Spying for the Man"

"Guys, take a seat. I'd like to have a word with you before you return to DSS." Jackson announced as the last of the group departed.

"You need me for anything?" Tabitha commented as she stood at the conference room door.

"No. Not at all. Just wanted to speak with my guys a minute about something. Good job up there." Jackson said.

"Thanks. I think it went pretty well." She said with a wave as she left the room.

"How do you guys think the meeting went?" Jackson inquired, as Justin and Rudy took a seat back at the table. "Look, within the IT department, you two are my boys. I trust you both as much as anyone. I value your opinion."

"Well…overall I think it went pretty well…but…" Rudy stated, trailing off at the end.

"But what?" Jackson pressed.

Rudy looked at Justin knowing he was about to say

something that could be conceived as negative about Tabitha and was a little concerned how his friend would take it. Regardless, he pressed forward realizing that the success of the project was paramount.

"I realize that Tabitha is perfectly capable of managing this effort to its conclusion, but she seems to be holding on pretty tightly to everything. I realize someone needs to drive this train, but Becky's point about having 'one belly-button' has some merit in my opinion. Tabitha's response seemed to indicate her reluctance to relinquish any control." Rudy stated still trying to choose his words carefully so as to not offend Justin.

"So, you're concerned about what could happen if Tabitha becomes…unavailable?"

"Yes sir…I suppose I am."

"Justin?" Jackson said casting a glace in his direction.

"I understand that concern, but I think it's a remote risk at best. She seems fully engaged to me and I see no reason to be overly concerned about it."

"Okay…anything else? Team leads level of engagement, for example."

"I can't speak for Rudy…" Justin said. "…but I was surprised by the seemingly genuine interest by the leads. I think there was some push back at first, but everyone, including Becky eventually saw the benefits."

Rudy nodded in agreement with his friend's statement.

"Okay, I don't want to keep you any longer. Keep me in the loop on any problems you consider as obstacles to this project's success. I don't want you to keep anything from me; not that I think you would; I just feel compelled to say that. Any issue you become aware of, I need to know about it…got it?" Jackson stated with a certain authority in his voice.

"Absolutely", they said almost in unison. Then the boys got up from the table and made their way out of the room, heading back to the DSS section. Once out in the hallway Rudy turned to Justin.

"What do you suppose that was all about?"

"Sounds to me like he wants us to be his Service Desk spies." Justin responded.

Chapter 4 Part 2

(May 6th)

On Friday morning Justin and Rudy sat in their office cubes

in the Desk Side Support section, working through the usual voice messages of customer IT issues. The antiquated customer outage reporting process had been outdated for some time and both were anxious to move on to the new Service Desk and Incident Management tracking software. The "process" of IT customers leaving voice messages for the IT staff describing their issues and hoping someone would work the issue would all be streamlined with the advent of the new Service Desk and its capabilities. The software vendor delivered the Incident Management software much faster than anyone anticipated and Justin and Rudy had already loaded it on the computers within the staged service desk area. But, now there was a roadblock to further progress.

"Hey Rudy." Justin yelled over in the direction of Rudy's cubicle.

"Yeah, what do you need, buddy?" Rudy responded while typing away at his keyboard.

"Have you spoken to Tabitha recently?"

"Umm, I think on Tuesday, why?"

"Well, I called her yesterday and it went straight to voice mail. We need some guidance before loading this software on other computers. I'm sure there is a license that dictates how many PCs we can load it on. Not to mention, when are we going to get the training on the software?" Justin stated.

"I hear ya. That's what I called her about on Tuesday." Rudy replied.

"…and?"

"Nothing. Honestly, when she answered it sounded like she had one too many, if you know what I mean. I just told her I'd call back later." Rudy said.

"She sounded like she was drunk?" Justin asked with surprise.

"That was my impression. Come to think of it, it did seem a little strange, now…when I say it out loud." Rudy stopped typing on the keyboard as he let the words sink in.

"Let me call her cell again." Justin said picking up his desk phone, while trying not to seem overly concerned.

The phone rang only once before going directly to voice mail. This was an indication her cell phone was either turned off or the battery had died. Either scenario was not indicative of Tabitha. Sure, she was a busy professional but to Justin's way of thinking, being a professional meant that at some point she would return the calls she had been getting.

"Well?" Rudy asked when he heard Justin place the desk phone back in its cradle.

"Straight to voice mail, again." He replied, now with a tone of concern clearly in his voice. With that, Rudy walked over to Justin's cube.

"You worried?" Rudy asked, seeing that his friend clearly was.

"I guess I am. But no reason to jump to conclusions. Maybe her cell phone is just on the fritz." Justin responded, in an effort to convince himself more than his friend.

"You know, maybe we should say something to the CIO about it. He did want us to inform him of any issues or concerns in the project moving forward. I think this qualifies." Rudy stated.

"I think you're right. Want to head up there now?"

"Sure. No time like the present."

They placed their phones on "hold" so any incoming customer calls would be routed to one of the three other DSS technicians. There were not many outages and calls probably because it was a Friday. It seemed many employees liked to "Check out" early or just take a day of vacation to extend the weekend. So Fridays were usually slow with the opportunity to catch up on things often placed on the back burner from earlier in the week. As they were leaving the DSS area on their way to the CIO's office, Justin popped his head into a co-worker's cubicle to let him know they would be away from their desks for a while. With a dismissive "whatever" wave, the co-worker continued surfing the internet and the boys headed for the CIO's office.

Chapter 4 Part 3

"Houston, We Might Have a Problem"

Mrs. Evans usually announced visitors coming to see Mr. Jones; in a sense acting as the gatekeeper to ensure he wasn't overly disturbed unnecessarily by other employees. She screened those who showed up unannounced and usually turned them away with only a distant appointment in hand for their trouble. However, Justin and Rudy were now considered "favored sons" of the CIO and it was common knowledge they were both welcomed to visit unannounced whenever they chose. This didn't sit too well with some of the other employees, especially the IT department, but Jackson Jones had taken both into his confidence in large part due to their performance in selling the project and their efforts to this point. Right now the boys could do no wrong in his eyes. They were somewhat oblivious to this special treatment and just assumed Jackson had an "open door" policy for everyone; which for the most part, he did not.

As they began walking the long hallway toward Mrs. Evans and the CIO's office she glanced up to see them approaching.

"Here come the little puppies." She said under her breath to no one but herself.

Internally she considered Justin and Rudy as the CIO's pets. This was for obvious reasons and she had overheard some other IT employees refer to the pair as pet employees of the CIO.

"We're going to see Mr. Jones, okay?" Justin announced.

"Hey, I just work here." Mrs. Evans responded rather curtly and out of character.

With that the boys gently tapped on the CIO's door. Upon hearing the response "enter," the two did just that.

"Hey there fellas, what's going on?" Jackson inquired looking up from his laptop while at the same time motioning for the two to take a seat.

The duo took turns explaining their concerns regarding Tabitha's availability…or lack thereof. Both tried to paint as untroubled a view as possible, but there was no mistaking the fact that the project was at a standstill until a few decisions were made. Although Jackson was tabbed to be Tabitha's backup that was only on paper and the CIO wasn't involved in the day to day managing of the project.

"By your estimation, how far behind are we on this project?" Jackson asked.

"Not very far…yet. There are a few tasks that are a couple of days behind." Justin began.

"But there are other future tasks that can't start until some of these delayed tasks get done. We don't want the delays to snowball." Rudy added.

"I understand your concerns and thank you for bringing this to my attention. When was the last time you called Tabitha?" The CIO inquired.

"Just a few minutes ago. Before we came to see you." Justin replied.

"Well, I'm sure it's nothing to be concerned about. Tabitha

is a board member and as such she doesn't work for me; so she may very well may be engaged by the board in some other capacity or working on something for the company president. Who knows, she may have just taken a few days and doesn't what to be disturbed. It wouldn't be the first time an employee needed some time off." Jackson concluded, all the while fully realizing his comments didn't address the problem the boys had come to see him about, since he didn't feel comfortable making the needed decisions himself. He continued.

"Either of you know where she lives?" Jackson inquired as they both shook their heads no. With a surprised expression Rudy looked to his friend since he figured if anyone knew where Tabitha lived it would be Justin, given their now obvious personal relationship.

"I'll get it from the company directory. I suppose it wouldn't hurt to swing by her place after work to speak with her and get the project back on track. I'll email you her address once I have it. Keep it confidential. Is there anything else?" Jackson inquired as a signal for the boys that he needed to move on to other pressing matters.

Justin and Rudy turned to leave and thanked the CIO for his time. Both headed back to the DSS section to finish what would turn out to be the remainder of an uneventful Friday work day.

Chapter 5 Part 1

"Clock Watching in DSS"

Toward the end of the day there were only two calls in the DSS queue and both went to Rudy. He passed one to Justin since they had both volunteered to stay the full day on Friday so their co-workers could get a jump on the weekend. Both jobs were simple password resets for absent minded or fat fingered employees that had either forgotten their network logon credentials or mistakenly entered the wrong password three times and found themselves locked out of their accounts. The customary procedure was to provide a temporary password that required the employee to change it once they were able to log on to their computer. Once in the system, both passwords were auto generated and the boys called their respective customers to inform them of the new passwords. Occasionally, the DSS technician waited on the phone while the customer ensured they could log in and change their password successfully. They both did so in this instance as there was little else to do while waiting for the end of the day. In most cases, once they provided the temp password, they would move on to other waiting customers.

"Well, what do you want to do now?" Rudy inquired, almost wishing for a few more outages to work.

"Sit here and watch the clock, I guess."

"Did you see the CIO's email with Tabitha's address? Doesn't look that far away." Rudy stated. "You've never been there?"

"Nope. She obviously knows where I live; but her address never came up." Justin responded.

"Doesn't look like it's very far from here…guess that's why Jackson wanted to meet there only 30 minutes after work." Rudy stated.

"Yeah, I looked earlier on-line to see how far it is from here. Looks like she's at the Willow Gardens Apartments off of Carpenter Avenue…Apartment 214."

"At least now you know where she lives in case you want to pay her a midnight visit someday." Rudy stated jokingly. He heard a muffled chuckle over the cubicle wall from his friend and was glad to hear it. Perhaps Justin wasn't as worried about Tabitha as he had seemed earlier.

Sneaking out early on a Friday at Southern United Insurance

Company for most employees had become routine. There seemed to be little, if any resistance, from leadership as long as the work got done. This turned out to be an unofficial perk of working for the company and leadership seemed reluctant to make an issue of it; especially since the practice has been allowed to continue unchecked for so long. On this day, Justin and Rudy would have probably joined the others looking for an early jumpstart to the weekend; but since they needed to meet Jackson at 5:30 at Tabatha's apartment, it made little sense to leave early. Departing from work and heading straight to her apartment was the obvious choice. Both killed the rest of the workday surfing the internet. Rudy spent the time checking baseball scores while Justin read the local news on one of the television station's websites. After a few minutes of mind-numbing internet distraction Rudy finally spoke up.

"Man, it's nearly 5. Let's get out of here. We can stop for a frappe on the way." Rudy suggested.

"Do you really want a frappe or do you just want to see Samm?" Justin replied.

"Both. I'll drive and I'll bring you back for your car once we're done at Tabitha's place."

"Fine with me. You're buying at Starbucks, right?" Justin responded, jumping at the opportunity to have his friend pull out his wallet for a change.

"Sure." Rudy stated.

The only thought that sprang into Justin's mind as the pair were leaving work was that his friend must be in love with Samm to put up zero resistance when asked to pay for something. The thought brought a smile to Justin's face as it was good to see Rudy open up more and he seemed much more confident and happy than in the past.

Chapter 5 Part 2

"That'll be Two Frappes to Go, Sweetie"

It was a short drive to the Starbucks and only 4 or 5 more blocks to the Willow Gardens Apartments after that. Starbucks wasn't exactly on the way, but it was close enough; and they did have a few minutes to kill anyway. When they arrived, Rudy pulled into the drive-thru primarily because he knew Samm was working the window today. She normally worked the overnight shift, but today she was filling in for someone. As they pulled up to place their order, Justin instinctively reached for his wallet.

"Hang on there cowboy..." Rudy said in his best John Wayne voice. "...this one is on me."

"My God, I must have died and gone to heaven." Justin said with a smile.

"Can I help you?" a distorted, almost computer like voice said as Justin and Rudy pulled forward.

"Hey Samm..." Rudy responded recognizing her voice immediately.

"Hi there Rudy...missed you today." She responded whispering quietly into her communication headset.

"Yeah, me too. Justin and I would like a couple of tall java chip Frappuccinos." Cluing Samm in on the fact that Justin was with him.

"Hi Samm!" Justin shouted into the drive thru microphone device.

"Justin. I didn't know you were there too. How have you been?"

"Super as always." Justin responded, sounding more chipper than usual.

As they pulled forward to the window to pick up their drinks, they could see Samm was already taking another order while another employee was busy making their drinks with lightning speed. As she accepted cash for payment for the drinks, she mentioned that she was still waiting for the phone call.

"I was planning to call you this weekend to set something up." Rudy responded intentionally loud enough for Justin to hear.

"You better, sweetie." She replied as she handed the drinks to Rudy along with his change.

Once out of the Starbucks drive thru, they knew it was time to meet up with Jackson over at Tabitha's apartment. Nothing was said between them until they were about half way to Tabitha's apartment. Then Justin turned to Rudy.

"Thanks for the frappe, sweetie."

"Shut Up!" Rudy responded as they both couldn't help but laugh at the exchange.

Pulling into the Willow Gardens Apartments, they noticed there was plenty of available parking. They drove around until they found the building marked 200. The building had only two floors whereas the other three buildings were three floors. This was a fairly new apartment complex. The clean white stucco of the building was bright in the late afternoon sun. The landscape was beautifully manicured with a child play area just to the left of building 200. Although not fancy by anyone's reckoning, it was a very nice and probably expensive place to live. As they pulled into a vacant parking space somewhere near the center of the building, they saw Jackson step out of his car.

"Hey guys. I see her car over there, so she must be home now." Jackson said as he walked over to meet the guys. Justin was surprised he hadn't noticed her vehicle when they first pulled into the parking lot.

"214 looks to be up there." Jackson said pointing over to the left corner on the 2nd floor. "The stairs are over there", he said as they all made their way to the left end of the building.

Walking to the stairs, Justin noticed a tall slender man heading toward the same set of stairs. He was dressed in Friday casual attire with jet black hair pulled back into a pony-tail. As the trio approached, it was clear he was heading up the stairs as well. Casual greetings were exchanged and the four men headed up the stairs to the second floor. Jackson, Justin, and Rudy headed to apartment 214. The man was right behind them and when they stopped in front of Tabitha's apartment, all three were surprised the pony-tailed man did as well.

"Excuse me, but are you here to see Tabitha?" The man inquired.

"Who the hell was this guy?" Justin thought. Maybe he was her boyfriend or another "friend with benefits." Little wonder she hadn't shared her address with him, he said to himself. Obviously she didn't want me walking in on her while she was entertaining someone else. His imagination clearly getting the better of him now.

"I'm Bruce, Tabitha's brother." The man offered.

Immediately Justin felt like a perfect ass for thinking such things about Tabitha.

Chapter 5 Part 3

"Horror Realized and the Implications"

Jackson was quick to speak up for the trio.

"My name is Jackson Jones. This is Justin and Rudy. We work with your sister. We've been trying to reach her for a couple of days, so we thought we'd come by and make sure everything was alright."

"Sounds like we're here for the same reason. My sister is a

brilliant person, but she can be a little scatterbrained at times." Bruce stated as he positioned himself in front of the door and knocked.

Fifteen seconds passed without a response from inside. Bruce put his ear to the door attempting to listen for any sound of movement within. He placed his hand over his other ear in an attempt to drown out the outside traffic noise.

"Nothing." He said as he knocked again while reaching into his pocket to pull out a single key. Obviously this was a spare key to his sister's apartment. He knocked once again harder this time and with more urgency. He placed his ear to the door, listening again for any sound that would indicate someone was inside. After a few seconds, he announced his intentions.

"Nothing. I'm going in." Bruce placed the key into the door lock.

As he unlocked and opened the door, all four men were overcome by the foul stench of decay that wafted from inside the apartment and mixed with the fresh outside air. All of them immediately knew something was horribly wrong inside the apartment but only Bruce seemed to suspect specifically what had happened as he rushed into the apartment in search of his sister.

Jackson, Justin, and Rudy were reluctant to enter at first until they heard Bruce scream from the back bedroom.

"Call 911!" He shouted.

All three quickly entered the apartment and eased closer toward the bedroom where Bruce's voice was coming from, but only Jackson continued to the bedroom doorway. Although Justin and Rudy had entered the apartment, both remained only a few steps inside the now open front door.

As Jackson stood in the doorway, he could see Bruce kneeling at the side of the bed and a motionless Tabitha lay on the bed. Bruce sensed Jackson's presence in the room and through subdued sobs, he turned to face Jackson.

"Please call 911! She needs help." Bruce pleaded as he turned back to his sister's lifeless body.

Jackson motioned to the boys to make the call as he stepped forward slowly to get a better look at Tabitha. Her face was ashen and her eyes were hazed and staring blankly into space. A syringe lay on the bed next to her along with some rubber tubing. She was in sweatpants and a red tank top with one shoe on while the other shoe was on the floor at the foot of the bed.

"Did you call for help?" Bruce inquired, the sobs beginning to ease.

"Yes. They are on their way." Jackson said reassuringly; not knowing for sure if the call had been made or not.

Jackson didn't have to examine her any further beyond his initial visual inspection to know she was dead. The life had drained out of her body hours ago and it appeared to be a drug overdose of some kind. Years earlier Jackson found his father dead in his home and the smell and visual signs of death were etched in his mind forever. For Tabitha, help would arrive much too late.

Jackson walked back to Justin and Rudy; allowing Bruce to grieve on his own terms.

"What happened?" Justin asked, even though part of him already knew the answer. Rudy had stepped outside to make the 911 call, and just then reentered the apartment.

"It's Tabitha. Looks like an overdose." Jackson replied.

Justin made a move toward the bedroom, but Jackson grabbed him by the shoulders before he could pass.

"Trust me, son. You don't want to see her like this." Jackson said like a father giving heartfelt advice to his son. "Rudy, take Justin outside and wait for the authorities."

Rudy put his arm around his friend and led him outside, down the steps and into the parking lot. Justin allowed his friend to lead him as if it were all just a bad dream.

Jackson walked outside to clear his nostrils and to contemplate what had just happened. Leaning against the 2nd floor railing, he thought of his father.

"Damn you! Why did you let the bastard win?" Bruce screamed at his dead sister. "You had him beat!"

Sobs returned, quietly, as the realization that his sister was gone finally sank in.

Chapter 6 Part 1

"Coroner and Rigor"

Seeing the sheriff's deputy pull into the parking lot, Justin and Rudy motioned to the open door on the 2nd floor. Making his way out of his cruiser, the deputy made his way up to the apartment where he met Jackson. The sound of an ambulance siren was heard in the distance, getting louder as it approached.

"What do we have here, sir?" The deputy asked.

Jackson looked up with a worn expression trying to wipe the vision of his dead father from his mind.

"There's a woman apparently dead inside lying on the bed." He replied not knowing what else to say to the deputy.

"Do you know who she is?"

"Yes. Her name is Tabitha Carson."

"Are you a relative?" The deputy inquired, jotting down information in his notepad.

"No. Her brother is inside with her. I'm…I mean…we're…her coworkers." Jackson explained pointing to Justin and Rudy who were looking up at the two men from the parking lot.

"I see. When did you discover the body?"

"Just a few minutes ago, I guess."

"You and your buddies hang tight for a few minutes." The deputy stated as he turned to head inside the apartment. Jackson thought about following him, but then thought better of the idea; seeing Tabitha dead once was enough for him.

Within a couple of minutes the siren of the approaching ambulance was suddenly gone; a clear indication that upon inspection of the scene the deputy had called in to inform dispatch the victim had passed and there was no longer a need for the response to be an expeditious one. After a few minutes later, the deputy coaxed Bruce from his sister's bedside to bring him outside; allowing the medics and the soon to arrive coroner space to do their jobs. While still asking questions to a shaken Bruce, the deputy eventually steered him toward a plastic chair that was outside a neighbor's apartment door. The deputy placed a reassuring hand on his back before returning to Jackson; still standing in front of the open doorway while keeping an eye on Justin and Rudy.

"So, you say you are a co-worker of the deceased?" The deputy said still making notes in his notepad.

"Yes." Jackson responded.

"Where you aware she had a possible drug problem?"

"No idea."

"Her brother said she'd been battling drug addiction for years. Hard to believe co-workers saw no visible signs." The deputy said rather matter of factly.

Jackson had to calm himself before he could respond. "Look, if I suspected for an instant anyone had a problem with drugs, I would've said something or took some action to help them."

"I understand sir. Just doing my job." The deputy said seeing Jackson was getting mildly upset. "What brought you over here today anyway?"

"No one at work had heard from her in a few days so we thought we should come and check on her."

"I see…I assume your boys down there will essentially say the same thing?" The deputy inquired motioning for Justin and Rudy who were still standing in the parking lot.

"I suppose…you'll have to ask them."

The silent ambulance, with lights flashing, finally pulled into the parking lot. A few curious onlookers began to poke their heads out of doorways to get a better look at what was going on once the ambulance arrived. Few stayed gawking very long once their curiosity had been satisfied. Most then retreated back into their own apartments to carry on with their daily routines. Even death has a short attention span for the living.

Two nondescript medics exited the ambulance, in no hurry, and pulled a gurney from the back of the ambulance, making their way up the stairs. The deputy met the medics as they arrived at the apartment door.

"Coroner on his way?" One of the medics inquired.

"Yes." The deputy responded.

All three stepped inside and the deputy let them to the back bedroom. Following standard operating procedures the medics checked Tabitha's vitals, but realized even before doing so that she was dead.

"How long, do you think?" The deputy asked almost absentmindedly, referring to how long she had been dead.

"That's a question for the coroner; but based on the condition of the body, I would guess 12 hours, maybe longer."

Jackson made his way down to the parking lot to wait with

the boys. He assumed the deputy would have more questions for them before they could leave.

"How are you doing Justin?" Jackson asked in a hushed tone as he approached the two.

"Okay, considering the circumstances."

"You and Tabitha…were dating?" Jackson inquired.

Justin thought only Rudy knew of his blossoming relationship with Tabitha and instantly looked at Jackson in complete surprise.

"Look, I hear things…it's important to know what's going on with my team."

"I guess you could say we were dating…but it was very early in the relationship. Neither one of us knew where it was headed." Justin responded with his head hung low.

"Are you going to be okay?"

Justin thought for a few seconds and responded.

"I guess I'll have to be. Won't I?" He said, still trying to rap his mind around the fact that Tabitha was now dead. Jackson placed a reassuring hand on Justin's shoulder.

"If you need anything, you can always talk to me." Jackson

said.

"Me too." Rudy chimed in.

"Thanks guys…appreciate it." Justin responded wiping the back of his hand over his face; trying to stem the flow of tears that had started and now were not going to stop.

While the trio was talking, they hadn't noticed a black car arrive and park. A large rotund man, looking disheveled and close to death himself, exited the vehicle and headed up to the apartment. He was inside the apartment only a few minutes before returning to his vehicle and driving away.

"I guess that was the coroner." Jackson said to nods of agreement from Justin and Rudy.

"Stay there…I'll be right down." The deputy shouted down to the trio.

Jackson gave an acknowledging wave.

The deputy returned to Bruce and whispered a few words into his ear, at which Bruce nodded yes. Then the deputy made his way back down the stairs.

"I need contact information from all of you before I let you go. It's standard procedure, in case we have any further questions.

It's doubtful, but you never know." The deputy said as he approached the men waiting in the parking lot. Jackson, Justin, and Rudy each took turns writing their names and phone numbers into the deputy's notebook.

"What about him?" Rudy inquired to the deputy referring to Bruce.

"Don't worry about him; I'll make sure he gets home okay."

The medics loaded the body encased in a black body bag strapped to the gurney and were in the process of bringing it down the stairs. Bruce never turned to watch as his sister was loaded into the ambulance. He just kept his head down waiting for the deputy to return.

"Okay, thanks. You're free to go." The deputy announced when his notebook was handed back to him after the men had finished.

"Yeah, let's go, Rudy, okay?" Justin said stealing a glance over at the gurney.

"You two take a couple of days off, but call me at work tomorrow." Jackson instructed. Both nodded that they understood his instructions.

Rudy led Justin back to the car and without another word spoken, they departed.

Jackson stood watching Tabitha being loaded into the ambulance while at the same time watching the deputy leading Bruce down the stairs. His mind flashed back to the memory of his father's death and with it came a single solitary tear trickling down his left cheek. He angrily wiped it away and headed to his car.

Chapter 6 Part 2

(May 13)

"Funeral for a Friend/Love Lies Bleeding"

Justin stood in front of his bathroom mirror struggling to adjust the black tie which hung loosely around his neck. He had to "Google" how to do it, since it had been years since the last time he was at a function that required a more formal attire than was his custom. However, this was a funeral for someone close to him and had things been different; perhaps they would have gotten much closer. He tried hard not to dwell on this as getting his tie just right seemed to require all his concentration and dexterity.

For some odd reason, all morning the Elton John song, "Funeral for a Friend/Love Lies Bleeding" kept playing in snippets in his head. He wasn't quite sure and didn't really know the words to the song, but it was one of those times when a song just gets stuck in your head like an earworm and you can't get rid of it. In this case he wished he could; as it just reminded him of Tabitha's death. He decided to attend her funeral since Rudy agreed to go as well. Had his friend not done so, Justin was certain he would have passed on her funeral. It would've been too difficult to go by himself. Rudy felt that as part of Justin's healing process, he needed to go to help find closure; regardless how many times Justin said he was fine; Rudy could tell his friend was still struggling to come to terms with the loss.

"Now, that doesn't look too bad." Justin whispered to himself as he finally got the tie to look acceptable. Putting on his suit jacket he was transformed into every bit the typical funeral mourner. With that, he heard a knock on his front door. He ran his fingers through his hair; walked briskly to the door to answer it. Upon opening the door his friend stood at the doorstep smiling.

"So, how are you doing?" Rudy inquired; also dressed in his "Sunday Best."

"I wish people would stop asking me that." Justin replied.

"Man, lighten up. I just meant it as a greeting…you know, like "good morning."

Justin had been asked repeatedly by his co-workers about his emotional well-being once news of his "relationship" with Tabitha had leaked out. Although deeply affected by the tragedy; and who wouldn't be, he was growing tired of all the concern for his welfare.

"Oh…yeah, sorry." Justin replied, smiling at himself for his overreaction to Rudy's greeting.

"Well, we should probably get going…the church is on the other side of town and we don't want to be late." Rudy said prompting Justin to grab his keys and wallet to walk out the door. As they departed Justin's apartment, Rudy led his friend toward his car and Justin, with his own car keys in hand, didn't object.

The drive to the little non-denominational church didn't take as long as Rudy had speculated and with unusually light traffic they made it to the church parking lot in twenty minutes. Once in the parking lot, they sat in the car without speaking for a while. As other attendees arrived Rudy and Justin scanned the parking lot looking for fellow employees they knew. Right away they spotted Mr. Ferguson, the company president, and Jackson Jones talking on the steps of the church. A woman, who appeared to be Mr. Ferguson's wife stood motionless beside him; waiting for her husband to finish the conversation with Jackson.

"Well, I guess we should go inside and find a place to sit." Rudy said, breaking the silence as he opened the driver's side door. Without responding, Justin opened the passenger side door and exited.

The church was small and quaint; looking like a hundred others you might pass while driving through the countryside. White brick with a tall steeple that seemed taller than it needed to be for the size of the church itself. It was surrounded by a beautifully manicured lawn with a white cross planted in the center of the lush green grass. As Justin and Rudy took in their surroundings as they made their way inside, the bell in the steeple began to chime; as if to suggest to those milling around outside that it was time for the ceremony to begin, signaling the final opportunity to pay their last respects to Tabitha.

Justin and Rudy found a spot in the back of the church just as the minister was making his way to the pulpit. They both were surprised at how few people were there. There were plenty of seats closer to the front, but Justin couldn't make himself go any further and he quickly sat down in one of the rear pews with Rudy following his lead.

"Is this what a person's life comes down to?" Justin whispered to himself. Rudy clearly heard him though he didn't respond. He could tell his friend was surprised that so few attended; and it saddened them both.

The minister went on for a few minutes talking about Tabitha in cryptic and rather generic terms that could have applied to almost anyone before finally asking if anyone wanted to come up to speak about Tabitha. Almost immediately, her brother stood up to indicate he wanted to say a few words. Sitting next to him in the first row were Tabitha's parents. Bruce walked slowly to the front of the church with papers in hand. He shuffled the papers for a moment before lifting his head to speak. The sound echoed through the sanctuary.

"Tabitha and I weren't as close as adults as we were when we were kids…as we get older and get on with our lives…who is? But that didn't diminish the love we had for each other…especially during her darker days. As some of you know, she had demons she struggled with for years…"

Pulling a handkerchief from his pocket he paused momentarily…then regained his composure.

"…I'm thankful she is at peace now. My mother and father did all they could to get her the help she needed…I guess sometimes everything we do isn't enough and God has other plans…"

Tabitha's mother and father were sobbing quietly now; overwhelmed at the loss of their daughter, but doing their best to keep it together. Justin, looking forward in their direction, couldn't imagine the pain they were experiencing. He turned his attention back to Bruce's words.

"…She would be particularly pleased at the generous and loving act by the Southern United Insurance Company to start a drug treatment and education foundation in her name…"

Bruce wiped the perspiration and tears from his face as he paused again.

"…at this time, I'd like to ask J. Roth Ferguson, the President of the Southern United Insurance Company to come forward." Bruce concluded, clearly happy to relinquish the pulpit to someone else. Mr. Ferguson came forward and seemed to stagger for a moment in his attempts to collect his thoughts.

"It is our pleasure to announce that in honor of Tabitha and in her name we will be starting the Tabitha Carson Drug Education Foundation. We are investing $700,000 to fund awareness and education programs for area high schools to teach them of the dangers of drug use. This is our small way of paying tribute to Tabitha and everything she meant to the company she held so dear…and to me personally. I'd like to think she is up there smiling now…while her passing is tragic…she will forever be linked to this foundation and the hundreds of young people it aims to help." Mr. Ferguson stated.

"Well that is a nice gesture, huh?" Rudy said, leaning over to his friend.

Justin nodded his agreement.

Tabitha's parents chose not to speak, but there were a few other friends of Tabitha who came forward to say a few words regarding their friend. Once everyone finished speaking the minister returned to conclude the service with a closing prayer. Afterwards he invited people to come forward to pray or simply say "goodbye" to Tabitha. It was an open casket.

"You going up?" Rudy inquired.

Justin hesitated for a moment and then rose from his seat in the back of the church.

"Yes I am." He stated, now firm and resolute in his decision.

He made his way to the front of the small church and took his place in the short line that had formed in front of Tabitha's casket. Bruce and his parents were at the front, with Justin somewhere in the middle of the line to say his goodbyes. He waited quietly, speaking to no one, as he inched closer. He looked around the church and noticed those that chose not to come forward were either mingling with each other or heading slowly toward the door to depart. He noticed Rudy was still sitting in the back of the church…waiting for him. It was at that moment; Justin fully realized just how lucky he was to have such a good friend in Rudy. A few steps closer now. As Justin and Rudy's eyes met from across the room, Rudy smiled, as if to reassure his friend. Justin inched up a few feet and suddenly realized he was next to view Tabitha. For an instant he thought about walking away, but knew if he did, he would regret that decision the rest of his life…so he stood fast. As the people in front of him moved on, Justin slowly walked up to the open casket.

He was struck by how beautiful she looked lying there in the coffin. It was true what they say; the dead look just like they are sleeping. The aroma of flowers surrounding the casket invaded his senses as he looked lovingly down to the peaceful Tabitha. She wore a simple white dress. A small gold cross rested motionless around her neck. Her face held no expression. He reached down to touch her hand, and was immediately repelled by the coldness of her skin. Summoning the courage; he touched her hand again; this time leaving it there. It took everything he had to fight the urge to pull away. He leaned close to Tabitha's face and whispered.

"Goodbye Tabitha. I love you."

Justin composed himself and slowly made his way back to Rudy.

Chapter 6 Part 3

"Endings and New Beginnings"

Rudy met Justin as he made his way to the rear of the church. As he approached, He stood up to meet him but said nothing. They headed to the door intending to go directly to Rudy's car and leave. Her family stood at the exit, thanking everyone for attending the service.

"Oh, gentlemen. Thank you so much for coming." Bruce stated, realizing who Justin and Rudy were and reaching out his hand to shake theirs. "This is our parents Don and Olivia."

"Thank you for attending…it was a lovely service, don't you think?" Olivia spoke; also offering her hand.

"Yes ma'am. Just beautiful." Rudy replied, realizing Justin hadn't quite recovered from saying his goodbyes to Tabitha.

"Did you know Tabitha well?" She asked.

Rudy looked at Justin, realizing he wasn't in a talkative mood, and responded for both of them.

"We were co-workers Mrs. Carson. We worked with Tabitha on a very important company project that she was the team leader on." Rudy continued, providing a rather generic response and not revealing anything regarding Justin or his relationship with their daughter. The line behind them was growing so Justin and Rudy moved down the church steps and into the parking lot. Neither said a word on the way to Rudy's car and nothing further was said until they were nearly back to Justin's apartment. Then Justin looked over to his friend and with one simple question, seemed to turn the page from the tragic past few days to the present task of picking up the pieces that were left behind.

"So, what do you think happens to the project now that Tabitha is gone?"

Rudy thought for a moment…happy his friend was considering the future…but uncertain of how to answer Justin's question.

"Man, I don't know. We were so close to having something in place that will make a big difference in our jobs…hell, everyone's job. What is it? Friday? I guess come Monday the CIO will have some sort of plan on how to move forward."

"Yeah, I can't imagine they'll let the project fall apart now. We're really not that far from rolling this out." Justin interjected.

"I would guess Jackson will figure out a way to move things forward over the weekend and we'll hear about it on Monday. We'll just have to wait and see, I guess." Rudy replied.

Justin nodded agreement as Rudy pulled into the parking lot of Justin's apartment complex.

"You want to do anything this weekend?" Rudy asked, still not 100% certain he should leave his friend alone.

"Not especially, I think I want to spend some time mapping

out what we need to do with this project…assuming it moves forward. I'll see you at work on Monday. Thanks for everything."

For the first time in days, Rudy got the sense his friend was "back." Although he knew Justin would never forget someone who meant so much to him, he could tell he had found a way to deal with it and go on with his life. He was glad of this, of course. But he still planned to find an excuse to call Justin over the weekend.

Chapter 7 Part 1

(16 May)

"A Breath of Life into a Dying Project"

As planned, Rudy called Justin Sunday afternoon to ask about his thoughts for the project moving forward; however he cared less about that and more about how his friend was doing. By all indications, Justin had done exactly what he planned to do over the weekend. He documented all tasks still needing to be completed in order to move the project to its conclusion. He was happy to share his thoughts with Rudy as they spoke on the phone.

--Communications campaign to advertise the new process employees will need to follow to seek assistance with IT problems.

--Assignment of personnel to the Service Desk

--Training on the new Incident Management tool.

--Develop processes (owned by the SD) on how to escalate incidents to the other IT sections when necessary.

--Develop other processes and reports as necessary (metrics reporting to leadership, etc.).

Justin confessed there were probably things he didn't think of but these were the big ticket items that needed to get done before the

Service Desk could go live. They both realized things were likely to crop up once they went live, but that was to be expected with any new venture. Rudy made note of Justin's list; so they would both be on the same page when; and if, they were called into Jackson's office to discuss the matter…and first thing on Monday they were.

As soon as they arrived Monday morning, Steve Parker, the DSS supervisor informed them Jackson wanted to see them in his office. Both headed up to his office knowing full well what this impromptu meeting would be about.

"Come on in guys. We've got some things to figure out." Jackson started as the boys entered and he continued typing away at his keyboard.

Justin and Rudy took their seats in front of Jackson's desk and waited for him to finish typing. Justin pulled out a little note from his pocket that had the activities he and Rudy discussed over the weekend. Justin showed it to Rudy and he nodded in agreement.

Just then Mr. Ferguson and Mr. Walton walked into the CIO's office and Jackson stop typing and look up. Justin and Rudy were surprised because they were not expecting the company president and a board member to attend.

"Good morning gentlemen." Mr. Ferguson announced as he entered the room.

He and Mr. Walton found seats and pulled them up to Jackson's desk.

"The Service Desk project...where do we go from here?" He stated as he sat down in the chair. Justin started to pull out his note with his plan of action scribbled on it, but thought better of it until his input was requested.

"First I think we need to decide whether we proceed, delay or scrap the project entirely; given that Tabitha was pretty much running the show. I don't think the last option is really an option at all given the money and resources we've already put into this project." Jackson chimed in.

"That's a fair, if not obvious assessment. Does a regroup or huddle make sense while we figure out how to proceed from here? Delay it to sometime in the future, I mean." Mr. Ferguson threw out to the group.

"I don't think so...neither does Justin." Rudy joined in rather unexpectedly. "We should forge ahead. Tell 'em Justin."

Justin slowly pulled the slip of paper from his pocket.

"I was thinking about this over the weekend and based on the tasks we still need to complete, we're not that far from standing up the Service Desk. Sure, we're going to miss some little stuff that we'll need to circle back later to address, but many projects run into that kind of stuff. Since 90% or more of the technical and hardware tasks are done, most of what still needs to be done is process and procedure issues..." Justin said, realizing he had everyone's undivided attention. He continued.

"...one of the first things we need to do is to communicate to the employees how they seek IT help going forward and specify when this will begin. Secondly, we need the names of those who will be assigned to the Service Desk. I'm not aware of any volunteers, so we'll need leadership involvement with this. Next, we get with the vendor on the Incident Management software training. Rudy and I loaded it on the desktops in the service desk and have played with the program a bit, but formal training on how to actually use it is vital to our success. Lastly, we're going to need to develop some Standard Operating Procedures (SOPs) the Service Desk people can use to guide them on how to do their daily duties. I see this as more fluid than the other items and it will probably change over time, but we need something to start with." Justin concluded, stuffing the paper back into his pocket.

"That's pretty impressive, young man." Mr. Ferguson stated.

"Well, we believe we're too close to implementation to delay it now…plus, I think Tabitha would want us to finish something she had started." Justin replied, surprised to hear those words come from him.

"Very true." Mr. Ferguson stated, nodding in agreement.

"So, who is on the hook to be the Service Desk Lead?" Mr. Walton inquired.

"I've got some candidates in mind. We'll make the announcement once we get closer to full implementation." Jackson stated.

"Fair enough. Okay, Jackson…it's your ballgame to play now. Go get it done. You have our full support." Mr. Ferguson stated as he and Mr. Walton got up to leave the office.

As soon as the two company senior leaders were gone Jackson turned to Justin and Rudy.

"You two never cease to amaze me." He said with a smile. "I've got a meeting in a few minutes. Let's chat tomorrow to formalize a plan to finish this up."

Chapter 7 Part 2

"Hatching a Plan for Success"

Later that day, Justin and Rudy sat in their cubicles developing a few slides to outline the plan to complete the final tasks required to implement the service desk project.

"What's the communication plan going to entail?" Rudy begun.

"I think there are a few things we can do to get this concept out to the masses. To start with someone from leadership could send out periodic email blasts to everyone in the company." Justin added to get the conversation started.

"Flyers are a good idea too." Rudy chimed in, as Justin jotted it down.

"What about a banner on the company home page? That's the default page everyone will see when they log in every day." Justin added. "Okay, that's a good starting point. We need an effective date, but that will be Jackson's call."

"Should we recommend who to actually assign to the Service Desk?" Rudy inquired, moving to the second point on Justin's list.

"I guess it wouldn't hurt to recommend some people…but ultimately that's not our call either."

Over the next few minutes they discussed the pros and cons of a few individuals being assigned to the new section; ultimately deciding on a recommendation from each section to move to the service desk based on each candidate's level of experience and likelihood they would be a good fit with the intent of the new service desk.

"Okay, as I recall the training was free when we purchased the software." Justin stated moving on to the third task on the list. "I've got the vendor's number here somewhere and I'll call to check their availability to conduct the training. They can do it in the Service Desk area as well any anyplace, right?"

"I don't see why not." Rudy responded.

"Okay, what about the type of SOPs we need to develop?" Justin said.

"Let me think about that back at my desk. I'll start putting the slides together and in the meantime you can call the vendor to check when they can get someone out here to do the training." Rudy suggested.

"Sounds like a plan."

Rudy went back to his desk to start putting the slides together for their next meeting with Jackson, while Justin searched his desk for the software vendor contact information. After a few minutes looking through scraps of paper, he found it. His heart sank for just a moment when he realized the handwritten note was Tabitha's. He held it tight for just a moment as the image of Tabitha raced through his mind, before placing it slowly and delicately on his desk as he reached for the phone; trying to stem the wave of sadness attempting to take control of his emotions. He dialed the number and flipped the note upside down and listened to the phone ringing on the other end. It rang three times before someone on the other end answered.

"Williams Software, Robert speaking. How can I help you today?" The voice on the other end asked.

Justin took a few seconds to push Tabitha out of his mind before responding.

"Anyone there?" The voice inquired.

"Oh, yes. This is Justin Smith from Southern United Insurance Company…we purchased some Incident Management software from your company a few weeks ago."

"Yes, of course. I worked with Tabitha Carson on that purchase." Robert responded.

"I guess you didn't hear, but she passed away recently, so I'll be your point of contact going forward." Justin interrupted before Robert could say anything else regarding Tabitha.

"I'm so sorry to hear that."

"Thanks, we're all pretty shook up over her loss…anyway; I'm interested in the IM software training we purchased. We'd like to get it scheduled soon." Justin said, moving the discussion back to the point of his call.

"…yeah, we can be pretty flexible. Just tell us what days you want, and we'll have a trainer out there." Robert responded.

"How many days is the training?"

"Two or three days depending on the number of students."

"What if we wanted a session for the SD and another one for the other sections? Two classes of 4 students each." Justin inquired.

"Okay, that would be total of 4 days…two days total for each class." Robert replied.

"Let me talk to my boss, we may want to start this as early as next week. Perhaps do one of the classes next week and the other class the following week."

"Not a problem. Just let me know what you decide." Robert stated. "Again I'm sorry for your loss."

"Thanks. I'll be in touch." Justin responded as he hung up the phone.

Justin jotted down what Robert had told him and he was glad the company could be so flexible in their training options. He knew the training was a critical step that needed to be done as soon as possible. He picked up Tabatha's handwritten note with the vendor's phone number again and placed it in his desk…still upside down.

Chapter 7 Part 3

"Plan Review"

After Justin made some additional notes regarding the training of the SD and other personnel, he walked over to Rudy's desk to check on his progress in putting the slides together.

"How is it going?" Justin asked.

"Not bad. What's the story with the training?" Rudy inquired pulling up a blank training slide.

Justin filled Rudy in on what the guy from Williams

Software had told him regarding their availability for training and Rudy added the information to the slide.

"That looks good. Let me see it from the beginning." Justin said, after watching Rudy create the new slide.

Rudy clicked the "slide show" button on the PowerPoint software and the presentation displayed in full screen on his computer.

Employee Communication Plan

- Periodic e-mail blasts from company leadership advertising the Service Desk and contact information
- Company Home Page banner
- Flyers posted throughout the building

SD Personnel Recommendation

- Diane Welch—DSS
- Tony Jackson—Servers
- Anthony Spicoli—Networks
- Carmen Benson--Phones

DSS	Servers
Networks	Phones

Incident Management Software Training

- Williams Software—training can begin as early as next week.
  - Will include all aspects of the training software and it's use.
    - How to document and manage reported incidents
    - How to pull metrics from the system
    - Routing tickets to other teams
    - Etc.

SD Process Development

- Service Desk Administration
  - Basic day to day operation of the SD
- Incident Handling
  - Process for handling reported incidents

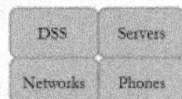

Service Desk Implement Date

- June 17th (Friday)
  - Mr. Ferguson should make first call to SD—symbolic show of support

Questions?

"Okay it looks pretty good, but I've got a couple of questions. How did you come up with those four people for the SD? Also, where did the 17 June date come from?" Justin inquired.

"Well, I thought about who might be available from each section and figured we wanted someone competent to handle the normal type outages, without wasting manning by placing a really highly skilled person into the SD. All these folks are fully trained in their respective sections, but as far as tenure within the shop…they are relatively junior. As for the date, I kind of just pulled it out of thin air. We have to draw a line in the sand to keep the date from constantly being pushed back." Rudy explained.

"I like your idea of having the company president make the first call to the Service Desk. Kind of like launching a ship by smashing a bottle of champagne across its bow." Justin replied. "I think we're ready to send it to Jackson and see what he thinks."

With a few keystrokes Rudy composed the email, attached the presentation file and sent it.

Chapter 8 Part 1

"…and the Work Begins."

(17 May)

Jackson opened the email from Rudy and clicked the accompanying attachment to begin reviewing the slides. He immediately noticed the short implementation timeline indicated on the slide.

"Only a month to get all this done?" He said to himself.

With only 4 or 5 major tasks left to get this project up and running, Jackson knew from past experience that things don't always go as smoothly as planned. He hoped the short project timeline could be attained, but he knew there were potential roadblocks, any of which could easily delay the start. Furthermore, he didn't understand why they chose a Friday to roll out something as important as the Service Desk. He would need to ask them to explain their logic on that decision. He did like the idea of having the company president make the first call to the Service Desk; although he wasn't sure what the call would be about. He wondered if Justin or Rudy planned to sabotage Mr. Ferguson's computer somehow so he would have to call in a reported problem. Surely not, he thought. There were a few missing details in that concept as well. After minimizing the presentation on his computer screen, he reached for his company cell phone.

"Justin, I was just reviewing your plan for the Service Desk and I have some questions. Can you and Rudy come up here?" Jackson inquired.

"Yes sir. We're on our way." Justin replied.

Chapter 8 Part 2

"Boys, You Have Some Explaining To Do"

It didn't take long for the boys to make their way to Jackson's office. This was becoming quite commonplace since they made the initial presentation and recommendation to stand up a service desk. More often than not, Mrs. Evans didn't give them a second look when they came walking down the hall. She usually gave most visitors strict scrutiny before allowing them into see the CIO. But she had long since realized it was best to allow Justin and Rudy the freedom to visit Mr. Jones whenever they needed.

Justin and Rudy gave her a friendly wave as they knocked lightly and entered.

"Guys, I appreciate you mapping this out…" Jackson said,

waving a hardcopy of the slides in his hand. "...but you need to explain a few things to me before I can buy off on it."

"Sure." Rudy responded as he and Justin found their customary seats.

"Let's start with why you are recommending these particular individuals to be assigned to the Service Desk."

Justin turned to Rudy to allow him to address this question.

"It really comes down to experience and seniority. We want techs that are fully qualified within their areas to tackle the basic calls coming into the SD. They were selected because we want to leave the more senior personnel in their respective sections, so they are available to work the more challenging jobs when those tickets get escalated from the Service Desk. Most of these people have no seniority and really only handle the basic stuff anyway, so it should have the least impact on each section." Rudy said, looking to Justin to see if he missed anything.

"Okay, I see where you are going here. I'll need confirmation from the department supervisors, but the selection criteria seems valid." Jackson responded, while looking through the slides for his next concern.

"Communication Plan. We're going to add a pop-up banner whenever an employee logs into their PC? I want employees to acknowledge they know this is coming. So, it'll be another form of advertisement to company personnel." Jackson stated. Justin and Rudy nodded agreement; surprised they hadn't thought of it.

"Explain to me how Mr. Ferguson making the first call would work." He asked.

"It's a symbolic show of support from the highest level of management. Either Rudy or I will be in Mr. Ferguson's office when the switch is flipped. We'll have him log onto his PC incorrectly three times so he'll automatically be locked out of the system. Then he'll make the call to the SD, the tech receives the call, on speaker of course, documents the call, re-enables his password, and closes out the ticket. Hopefully with the other SD folks on hand to watch how simple the process works." Justin said.

"I like it…but I don't like the timeline. A month doesn't seem like enough time to get everything done."

"Granted, it could slip, but we had to pick a start date. And we think this one is achievable." Rudy interjected.

Jackson nodded his head in agreement. "What do you need

from me?"

Rudy and Justin looked at each other for a moment before responding.

"Sir, we need your leverage to get the people assigned to the Service Desk." Justin stated.

"Done. It may not be the four you named, but you'll have them. What else?" Jackson asked, while jotting down his to-do list.

"Training…these people need to be available for training next week when the vendor arrives. Additionally, one more person from each IT department will receive the training. Class is only 2 days long." Rudy said.

Once again Jackson nodded agreement as he scribbled…then looked to Justin and Rudy for the next issue.

"I can draft the announcement pop-up you were talking about and get it to Becky on the Server team to deploy." Rudy offered.

"Good. Keep it short and sweet…we want folks to read it." Jackson said. "Justin, you'll call the vendor to get the training scheduled?"

"Tuesday through Friday of next week should work." Justin replied

"Make it happen." Jackson said.

"I'll take care of the flyers and have Mrs. Evans distribute them throughout the building." Jackson added.

"Anything else?" The CIO asked, primarily himself. "Process…what's the story with that?"

"That's going to be a fluid endeavor, documents and standard operating procedures require modification from time to time, but Rudy and I will put some initial drafts together for the Service Desk to use initially." Justin said.

"I'll send an e-mail announcement out to the team with everything we've discussed. Any questions? Let's get busy." Jackson announced as a queue for the boys to return to work.

Chapter 8 Part 3

"The Cat is Out of the Bag"

(18 May)

When Justin and Rudy arrived the following morning, one of the first things they noticed was the new login pop-up.

<u>Effective on or about 17 June, please call extension 4000 for any IT related incidents. DO NOT call individual IT sections or personnel to work your IT problems. The NEW Service Desk will be</u>

<u>the owner of all customer IT problems.</u>

"How does that strike you?" Rudy asked, knowing Justin already logged in and must have seen it.

"It looks good. Did Becky give you any static about it?"

"No. Actually she was pretty accommodating." Rudy responded.

Once Justin logged in, he opened his email and saw the new email from the CIO. It was addressed to IT TEAM_ALL. He opened it and began to read.

IT Team,

As most of you know, we've been working an initiative to better serve our company employees/customers by streamlining the way we handle incidents and IT outages. Part of that strategy was the implementation of a project to stand up a Service Desk. Due to the passing of the project's manager, Tabitha Carson, I've appointed Justin Smith and Rudy Vargas as co-PMs to see this project to completion. You are to give them all required assistance to make this happen. We are shooting for a go live date of 17 June and are hopeful, with everyone's assistance, this can be accomplished. After consultation with the IT section supervisors, the following individuals have been selected to be the inaugural team assigned to the SD effective with the go live date:

Diane Welch—DSS

Tony Jackson—Servers

Anthony Spicoli—Networks

Carmen Benson—Phones

Service Desk supervisor will be assigned at a later date.

These individuals are assigned to attend training next week on the new IM software we purchased from Williams Software. This software will be a game changer for us. It will allow us to track outages over time and perform analysis on reported outages. This capability brings us closer to doing real Problem Management going forward; and eliminating recurring incidents we see every day. We will schedule additional personnel to attend this valuable training in the weeks to come, and I ask supervisors to be flexible to allow people from your shops to attend.

This project has company president and board level interest, and will be successful. We require everyone's best effort to make this a reality. This is the precipice of a significant transformation for our IT department; and I encourage your support and participation.

I will continue to provide updates as we progress.

v/r

J.J, CIO

Southern United Insurance Company-HQ

    Justin read the e-mail and he was glad the CIO specified a number of items that needed the IT team's commitment, but he was confused by one particular statement.

    "Rudy, did you read Jackson's e-mail yet?"

    "Just finished." Rudy responded.

    "Project Managers…really." Justin asked.

    Rudy walked over to Justin's desk.

    "Weren't we pretty much the PM's for this effort all along…not to mention the Lead Technical Experts? I think Jackson just formally named us as PMs to reduce any backlash we might encounter from this point on." Rudy explained.

    "I guess you're right. Who do you think will be named the Service Desk Lead?" Justin inquired.

    "Who knows…probably an outsider who'll know nothing about how we operate."

    Both chuckled at the statement primarily because they knew

it to be true. Whenever there was a management vacancy in the company, rather than hiring and promoting from within, the powers that be always seemed to bring in an outsider with "a fresh look" to make improvements or corrections to what leadership perceived was wrong.

Chapter 9 Part 1

"Training Day"

(24 May)

When Justin walked in to work the next day he saw Mr. Sparks, the Williams Software trainer well into the introductory lesson for the new IM Software. All four projected Service Desk employees were busy scribbling notes as fast as Mr. Sparks could talk. It was good to see the new Service Desk people so engaged in the training. He felt confident the selections were the correct ones. Justin paused in the SD area for just a second as the lesson proceeded. Mr. Sparks, whom Justin met late last week, gave him a nod of his head without skipping a beat in the training presentation.

A podium was set up next to the four SD workstations and training slides were displayed on a temporary projector screen. Justin wasn't sure how the set up worked exactly, since Rudy took care of the technical issues to satisfy the trainer's IT requirements. It appeared Mr. Sparks was explaining how to create a ticket for a new customer call (outage). While Justin listened it appeared he was discussing outage priorities. Not wanting to become a distraction or a gawker, Justin moved on to the DSS area where he planned to meet

Rudy to see what needed to be done today.

"Looks like the training is going like gang-busters." Justin mentioned as he passed by Rudy's cubicle on his way to his desk.

"Yeah, even though it's in an open space, it's working well. I was there when Mr. Sparks started, then I booked once I saw everything was going smoothly." Rudy replied.

"What's on the agenda for today?" Justin asked.

"Setting up the other half of the training…for the sections. I saw Jackson sent out another email today. He's really doing his best to keep this front and center." Rudy said.

"Give me a minute…let me read his email." Justin announced.

IT Team,

In my previous email, you may recall I mentioned the vital nature of the Service Desk project and specifically the newly-assigned Service Desk Techs attending training to learn how to maximize the benefits of the IM tool. Training started this morning and will continue for the next few days. If you have business in the DSS/SD area, I ask that you be quiet while passing through. Due to the need to have training take place within the spaces the SD techs will occupy when we go live, this is considered to be an open environment. Additional training will take place for select other members of the IT staff at a later date. If you are selected, you will be required to provide on-the-job (OJT) training to other members of your section. We remain on track for a 17 June launch; and I ask you to remain steadfast in your support for this extremely vital company mission enhancement.

v/r

J.J, CIO

Southern United Insurance Company

"How about a coffee?" Justin asked as he finished reading Jackson's email.

"I thought you'd never ask." Rudy replied.

Chapter 9 Part 2

"Break Time"

They locked their computers and headed to the cafeteria to get a couple of their now "famous" mochas. With their drinks in hand, they found a table by a window overlooking the parking lot.

"Say, did you ever have that date with Samm?" Justin asked, quite nonchalantly.

"What did you say?" Rudy replied, although he heard exactly what Justin asked.

"Remember when we went to the Starbucks before going over to…you know Tabitha's. Samm gave you her number and wanted you to call to set something up, right?" Justin explained, as he took a sip of his drink.

"Well…as a matter of fact, we did have a date. Went to see a movie together." Rudy said with a sly smile.

"Really?"

"Yep, in fact we're been out to dinner too." Rudy said.

"Sounds like you've been holding out on me." Justin said, now fishing for more details.

"Well, things look promising but I wasn't sure you were ready to hear about it just yet…with Tabitha…you know…" Rudy said, his voice trailing away.

"Don't worry about it. I need details." Justin said. He was happy to hear the good news about Rudy's blossoming relationship with Samm. There was no longer any reason for such news to send Justin into a dark funk about his relationship with Tabitha.

"We just went to some "chick flick" movie she wanted to

see. I didn't care for it much, not enough car chases or buildings blowing up. But it was nice. Since we didn't get much of a chance to talk at the movie; a couple of days later we had dinner together…" Rudy continued as Justin listened with a certain eagerness for more information.

"…so we could…you know…just talk to one another. You know she doesn't just work at Starbucks. She's in school learning Occupational Therapy. She wants to help people with injuries or illnesses that require them to have to learn to walk again."

"Sounds like you have a winner my friend." Justin chimed in.

"Yeah, hard to believe she wants anything to do with me." Rudy said.

"No kidding. She could do a whole lot better than you." Justin said with a smile. Both chuckled at the comment. "So, when do you see her again?"

"I told her with this ongoing project, I'd be a little busy, so probably once the Service Desk is fully operational. She was okay with that. She even wants to take me somewhere special to celebrate once things slow down."

"Good. Just don't screw things up…I'm really happy for you."

"Thanks. That means a lot."

"Okay, want to get back to the project?" Justin inquired as Rudy nodded in agreement. "I need to make arrangements for the second training session for the non-SD personnel and you can start on the SOPs. What do you think of that?"

"That's fine, but these SOPs are going to be tough to put together." Rudy admitted.

"We just need the basics for now…something they can use to get the ball rolling. SOPs are a living document and need to be modified from time to time. That will for be the Service Desk supervisor to address down the road…whoever that turns out to be."

"Okay…as long as you don't think they need the whole song in the SOP and can be useful with only the first verse, I can handle that." Rudy replied.

"I'll help out too, once I get the second training class scheduled." Justin assured his friend. "I'll send an email to Jackson with an update on where we are and copy you on it. I think we're on schedule to make the deadline."

With the conversation at an end, they headed back to their desks.

Chapter 9 Part 3

"All Things Proceeding as Planned"

Justin realized he had a couple of quick emails to send before he could help Rudy with writing the SOPs for the Service Desk.

Mr. Jones,

I wanted to give you a quick update on our progress. As you know, the first round of training for the selected SD personnel is underway and should wrap up tomorrow on schedule. I will be working with the other IT section leads to select personnel to attend the next round of training...likely next week. Since the SD area isn't yet being used operationally, the plan is to use the space for the second round of training; since there have been no significant issues of note.

Rudy and I have started working on a baseline SOP(s) the SD can utilize at start up, but there will certainly need to be modifications to these documents going forward as the day to day operations of the SD become clearer. In my view, that is a task for the new SD Lead. This should be the last piece to be accomplished prior to going live. The SD will be a work in progress even after it goes live, but I believe we are still on track to implement on 17 Jun.

Thanks,

Justin Smith, DSS

Justin addressed the email to Mr. Jones and copied Rudy; then sent it. He opened another blank email and started writing. This one was addressed to Steve, Marcus, Becky, and Paul; the current IT section leads…copying Rudy and the CIO.

IT Section Leads,

As you are well aware, we have started the training required for the new individuals selected for the SD assignments. In line with that, I'm working with the vendor to set up another training session for one member from each of your sections for next week 1-2 June. Once these people have been through the vendor training they will be responsible for providing OJT for the other members of your teams.

Please nominate someone from your teams to attend the training so I can provide a list of who will attend to Mr. Sparks (Vendor trainer). Please reply with names by COB today so I can make arrangements with the vendor. You are aware of the CIO's recommendations for this training. Thank you and if you have any questions, please let

Rudy or I know.

Thanks,

Justin Smith, DSS

    Justin read through the email a couple of times to ensure it didn't sound too formal. Once he was satisfied, he hit send and went to help Rudy with the SOP development.

Chapter 10 Part 1

"SOP: Stinking Operating Procedures"

(27 May Friday)

"These SOPs are like an onion the size of a watermelon and the more you peel back a layer, the stinkier it gets." Rudy complained.

Rudy had come in early the last few days to work on the last of the SOPs, which he was having some difficulty completing. The other SOP regarding Incident Reporting and Documentation he found to be relatively easy since he had the vendor's training documentation to draw from. The SOP regarding the day-to-day operation of the Service Desk was quite a different animal all together. This was the SOP he seemed to be having the most trouble with.

As Justin walked in and passed Rudy's desk on this Friday morning, he could quickly tell his friend was pulling his hair out. Justin knew he needed to lend a hand to keep Rudy from going off the deep end.

"You need a hand with anything?" Justin asked as he stood next to Rudy's desk.

"Man, do I." He gladly announced, clearly in need of a helping hand.

"Okay, let's see what you've got so far." Justin said pulling up a chair to sit next to Rudy.

Rudy brought up the Service Desk Day-to-Day Operations SOP table of contents so Justin could see where he was trying to get to.

TABLE OF CONTENTS

1. RESPONSIBILITES
    a. SERVICE DESK LEAD
    b. SERVICE DESK TECHNICIANS
2. PROCEDURES
    a. STANDARDS OF CONDUCT
    b. MASTER STATION LOG
    c. READ BOARD
    d. PERSONNEL INDOCTRINATION
    e. TRAINING
    f. ESCALATION PROCEDURES

"So, you see my problem?" Rudy asked while looking at Justin with glazed over eyes.

"Other than not knowing what a READ BOARD is…not really. Seems pretty workable to me." Justin replied.

"You don't think it's pretty thin? I mean, if we covered everything the Service Desk does or will do, this could take forever to document properly." Rudy explained.

"Yeah, that's the point; we don't need to cover everything. The new SD supervisor will put the bells and whistles in the SOPs. You've got the Incident Reporting SOP done, right?" Justin inquired.

"That was pretty easy actually. All that was required was stepping through the processes of documenting the outages. I used the vendor docs to create it." Rudy explained.

"Okay, that's the big one anyway. Send it to me and I'll read it over to make sure it makes sense and you didn't miss anything. So, what is a READ BOARD anyway?" Justin inquired.

"It's like a knowledge capture mechanism where the SD techs can capture…a better way of doing something or solving a common customer problem and share the knowledge with other SD techs and IT departments." Rudy explained.

"Sounds like a good idea." Justin said as he headed over to

his desk to begin reading the Incident Reporting SOP. "You good now?"

"Yeah, I'll just keep things basic…I got it." Rudy responded, relieved he didn't need to venture as far into the weeds as he initially thought.

Chapter 10 Part 2

"It Sure Looks Pretty"

(7 Jun Tuesday)

With only ten days remaining, Justin walked in to work that morning, as he did every morning. Rudy arrived at the same time and they both stopped to look at the new Service Desk area before heading to their desks. The SD cubicles were unoccupied and looked pristine with all new computers and monitors barely used during the two training sessions. From a technical standpoint, all that remained was to turn on the equipment and get the personnel in place on the 17th to start managing the calls.

"Everything looks good, don't you think?" Rudy asked while still admiring the virtually untouched workspace.

"Yeah, makes me feel proud of what we accomplished." Justin replied.

"Think there'll be another bonus in it for us?" Rudy asked somewhat jokingly.

"Hell, who knows around here." Justin replied. "We still have to meet with Jackson to go over last minute stuff this morning, but I think we are ready; don't you?"

Rudy paused a moment before responding; apparently thinking back to everything they had accomplished for the big cutover on the 17th.

"I'm sure we've missed some stuff along the way, but all the big ticket items we got down cold...yeah, I think we're ready." Rudy said, with an air of confidence he rarely displayed.

The boys set about the workday still using the soon to be forgotten "old school" methods of handling customer IT complaints...checking their voice mail accounts for customer complaints of IT services that were not performing up to par. At this point, based in part on the ongoing ad campaign; everyone in the IT department (for the most part) now believed the implementation of the Service Desk and the new outage handling procedures would make everyone's life much better; to include the customers/employees that reach out to the IT department for services. For most, the 17th couldn't come fast enough. Justin and Rudy took care of the customer calls waiting for action within their respective voice mail accounts…knowing there was a much better process starting in the very near future.

Chapter 10 Part 3

"A Meeting of the Minds, with Nothing to Discuss"

Justin and Rudy made their way to Jackson's office knowing; or certainly suspecting, there would be little to discuss and expecting this to be more of a "feel good" meeting so the CIO could pass on to the president and board members the news that everything was on track and assure them the deadline for implementation would be met. As they entered the CIO's office, they noticed Mr. Jones standing in front of his office window staring out into the parking lot and beyond.

"Sit down, boys." Jackson said without turning around; somehow sensing the two had entered his office. "I want to show you something."

Jackson turned face to the boys and headed back to his desk. Reaching under his desk he pulled out a large rectangular piece of wood roughly two feet by one and a half feet. He flipped it so the front of the wood could be seen by the boys.

The Tabitha Carson Memorial Service Desk

The boys quickly realized it was a plaque Mr. Jones intended to display somewhere in the Service Desk area to honor the memory of Tabitha for all the work and dedication she had given to the project's success.

"Well, what do you think?" Jackson asked them.

Rudy immediately thought it was an outstanding idea, but he was slow to speak preferring to allow Justin to answer first. Rudy looked over to his friend; awaiting his reaction.

"I'm surprised I didn't think of something like this. Outstanding idea, sir." Justin said without further elaboration.

"I agree. It's a very cool thing to do." Rudy said, echoing his friend's sentiments.

"Okay…I only needed to confirm this was something…well, appropriate to do, under the circumstances. On to more pressing matters…" Jackson stated as he tucked the plaque back under his desk. "…What is left on the agenda? Sounds like we are ready to go, correct?"

"I think so. We have something like nine or ten days until

the 17th to catch anything we missed, but I think we're essentially ready to go live." Justin said confidently.

"But, there will need to be some clean-up and adjustments along the way for the Service Desk lead. I'm sure we're going to find the need to modify some things we just don't know and can't know until we actually turn the service on." Rudy said, wanting to ensure Jackson was aware there would still need to be some work done after the 17th.

"I think everyone understands that; and I'm sure the new Service Desk lead will be on top of it." The CIO said with a strange and wry smirk.

"I think those email reminders you are sending should continue and include everyone in the company…not just the IT department." Justin stated.

"Way ahead of you…Mr. Ferguson is going to start advertising the SD and process for requesting services later today and continue until the go live date. I think most everyone in the company understands what is coming with the flyers all over the place and the log on script coming up every time they log into the computers." Jackson explained.

"What about the plans for the go live date?" Rudy inquired.

"Glad you asked…" Jackson said with a smile. "…Justin you will be in the President's office at 10AM and assist him with making the first call to the Service Desk."

"Got it…I'll ask him to lock out his password and he'll call the Service Desk to have his password reset. It should go smoothly." Justin confirmed.

"Rudy, you'll be down in the SD with me…most of the IT department personnel will be there as well; company leadership, other department heads and others will be there. So, Rudy your job will be to ensure this demo goes smoothly…make sure the person answering the first call can fix the President's problem…and be sure the call is on speaker so everyone can hear how it goes. Justin, you and Mr. Ferguson will come down after the service call and we'll have a little celebration…snacks/punch…something along those lines. I'll see to it."

Justin and Rudy both nodded in agreement.

"This should take only a matter of minutes if everything goes according to plan and should illustrate the true impact the Service Desk will have on our IT operations. Anything else?" Jackson asked, giving the boys one last opportunity to raise any potential concerns.

Since they could think of no other significant issues standing in the way of the planned implementation date, they excused themselves from the CIO's office and went back to work; knowing they were as ready as they could possibly be.

Chapter 11 Part 1

"Jun 17th: A Time of Change"

Justin arrived at 9AM on what was expected to be one of the most significant days in the company's history. He wanted one final check of the Service Desk. And he wanted to ensure everyone was in place; with no unexpected surprises to prevent the SD implementation. He saw more employees milling around the Service Desk area than he anticipated. Jackson Jones was chatting with a few other company seniors. Justin could clearly see Jackson was carrying a large item under his arm, almost certainly the plaque he revealed to them a few days earlier. It was wrapped, so as to hide what was written on it, but based on the shape, he was certain it was the plaque. Justin looked over to the four techs now sitting in their assigned seats in the Service Desk area and immediately noticed Rudy speaking with Diane Welch. She was the DSS rep assigned to the Service Desk and she would undoubtedly be the person to take the call from Mr. Ferguson, the company president, who would ceremoniously make the first call with a simple network password problem. Rudy was speaking with her and pointing at a few things on her dual monitors at her assigned station. Justin thought about walking over to see what was going on, when he heard his name called out from behind him.

"Justin!" Jackson waved him over.

His attention temporarily diverted from Rudy and the Service Desk, Justin quickly walked over to Jackson and the person he was speaking with.

"Yes sir?" Justin inquired as he approached the two men.

"Justin, this is Sam Packard, the VP of Claims."

Justin reached out to shake the man's hand. He had seen him in the building before but didn't know who he was or what position within the company he held.

"Justin, your boss here tells me we have you to thank for this effort. I can't tell you how important the IT systems and software are for the claims folks upstairs. They used to complain all the time about the lack of responsiveness when something went down. To have a single point of contact into the company's IT world is a game changer for all of us." Mr. Packard said, clearly happy with the potential positive impact the venture would have on his claims staff.

"Thank you sir, but I had a lot of help. Rudy was a big part of it as well." Justin said trying not to absorb all the praise being heaped on him.

"I plan to say something to him too, believe me." Mr. Packard replied.

"Shouldn't you be getting up to Mr. Ferguson's office?" Jackson said as he looked yet again at his watch.

"I was going to see if Rudy needed a hand."

"I spoke to him earlier…I think he has things under control." Jackson said, assuring him everything was in capable hands.

As Justin turned to head up to the President's office, he ran into Steve Parker, Justin's current direct supervisor and the lead of the DSS section.

"Well, looks like you pulled it off" Steve said as they approached.

"I hope so, but it's not a done deal yet."

"I'm proud of you. Be sure you come back down after Mr. Ferguson makes the phone call." Steve said.

"Sure." Justin replied, thinking he had nowhere else to go.

Steve patted him on the back before they turned to head in opposite directions. Justin continued toward Mr. Ferguson's office while Steve walked into the growing crowd of employees around the

Service Desk and disappeared.

Chapter 11 Part 2

"The First Service Desk Call"

As Justin approached Mr. Ferguson's office, he noticed the door was open. Before he could announce his presence in the doorway, Mr. Ferguson waved him inside.

"Justin take a seat while I finish up something." Mr. Ferguson said while only briefly looking up to acknowledge his arrival. Justin sat quietly waiting for Mr. Ferguson to finish up whatever he was working on. After what seemed like an extended period of time, but in fact was only 5 minutes or less, he started to get impatient sitting quietly in the president's elaborate office. Mr. Ferguson finally looked up at Justin and spoke.

"I bet you're a little nervous today, right?"

"Yes sir." Justin replied.

"From what I hear everything is going like clockwork…have you heard anything otherwise?" Mr. Ferguson inquired.

"No sir. I'm not aware of any issues likely to pop up." Justin replied.

"We should be fine, then…listen, son, there is something I

want to tell you, since we have a few minutes." Mr. Ferguson stated, capturing Justin's undivided attention. "...when Tabitha died, immediately I felt it was in the company's best interest to scrap or certainly delay the project until we could properly evaluate its leadership needs. My gut told me this project, although far along, was without leadership when it was needed most. Had it not been for Jackson's confidence in you and Mr. Vargas to bring everything to a successful conclusion, I certainly would have scrapped it. Jackson thinks very highly of you two; and I'm inclined to agree with him. I'll also say we see big things in your future here."

Justin wasn't sure what his final comment meant exactly. He wanted to ask for further explanation; but ultimately figured he must be referring to another bonus of some kind.

"Thank you, sir. Speaking for both of us, it means a lot that you and Mr. Jones have so much confidence in us."

"Okay, we're getting close to the magic hour...what do I need to do?" Mr. Ferguson asked.

Justin explained all he needed to do was attempt to log in three times with a wrong password so his network account would be locked; thereby creating a need to notify the Service Desk for help.

Mr. Ferguson did as instructed and on the 4th attempt a login banner appeared with the message, "Notify the IT department for assistance."

"We need to change this to state 'Notify the Service Desk for assistance.'" Mr. Ferguson quickly observed.

Justin took the small notepad from his pocket and scribbled a reminder to make the correction. Then he pulled out his cell phone and called Rudy to check to see if everything was in place for the ceremonial first call. Rudy answered on the first ring and immediately informed Justin everything was in place and they were ready.

"Sir, its go time. They are ready when you are." Justin informed him.

Mr. Ferguson reached for his desk phone and made the call to the Service Desk.

"Hello, this is Mr. Ferguson and I'm having a problem logging into my computer…the system is telling me my password is locked. Can you help me with this?" He inquired, as if reading from a script.

The call was handled by Diane since she was the DSS rep in

the Service Desk. The phones within the Service Desk were set up in a rather traditional hunt group configuration where if one line was busy, it would automatically roll over to the next available line until it found a free line to ring. In this case the other three techs placed their phones in "busy" mode so the call would go to Diane, as the only available phone. As instructed she immediately placed the call on "speaker" so those gathered around the Service Desk could hear the interaction.

"Yes sir. I can help you with that. Please stand by while I bring up your log in credentials." She instructed.

Diane already had the incident management software open on her left monitor and the network access program on the right monitor. After a few key strokes and a click on her mouse, she unlocked his account.

"Sir, please try to log in again with your normal username and password." She instructed.

After 30 seconds of silence, Mr. Ferguson responded.

"I'm in…thank you for your help." He responded.

"You are welcome, sir. Can I help you with anything else?" She said.

"I'm good. Thanks." Mr. Ferguson stated before disconnecting the call.

A quiet smattering of applause began to rise as it became clear the demonstration; although staged, was a success. Rudy pointed to Diane's left monitor and reminded her to complete the incident ticket documentation, and she nodded in concurrence. Rudy looked over to Jackson and he gave Rudy a smile and a "thumbs-up" gesture. He let out a deep breath and thought about where Samm was planning to take him in celebration of the successful Service Desk project completion. He didn't really care where they went; but he was looking forward to more time with her now with the project completed. He would have more free personal time.

Meanwhile up in Mr. Ferguson's office:

"Sounds like it went exactly as planned."

Justin was clearly relieved and felt as if the weight of the world had been lifted off his shoulders.

"We better head downstairs for the festivities, don't you think?" Mr. Ferguson said as he got up from behind his desk. Mr. Ferguson put his hand on Justin's shoulder as the two of them exited the office together. As they walked down the hall toward the elevators, Mr. Ferguson said, "I'm proud of you, young man."

Chapter 11 Part 3

"The Unexpected Surprise"

When they arrived in the Service Desk area, Mr. Ferguson gave Justin a pat on the back for a job well done, then turned to meet Jackson and other company seniors. What caught Justin's eye more than anything else was seeing the Service Desk technicians all on the phone; clearly taking real calls and creating actual incident tickets; presumably helping customers and other employees solve their IT issues. He spotted Rudy standing alone in a small area off to the side of the Service Desk.

"I guess everything worked out, huh?" Justin asked as he approached Rudy.

"Yeah, and real calls are coming in." Rudy said pointing to the techs on the phone.

"I saw that. There are probably a bunch of employees who've been sitting on non-critical issues for some time now. Since the Service Desk provides them an avenue to report them; they are calling in." Justin explained

"That makes sense." Rudy said.

"Everyone gather around, please." Jackson announced; trying his best to be heard over the many individual conversations now going on. He repeated his announcement a second time but much louder and everyone began to move closer.

"I'm glad you could all take a few minutes out of your day to witness something that will prove very beneficial to the entire company. We have a few announcements to make before we cut the cake." Jackson said as he handed the covered plaque to Mr. Ferguson.

"As most of you know, Tabitha Carson passed away a few weeks ago. Without her steadfast dedication the project may not have succeeded. So, in honor of her efforts and her memory, we wanted to do something special." He said as he unwrapped the item Jackson gave him.

He held it up, showing it to the crowd. Everyone cheered and applauded.

"We are going to find a suitable place to display this so we never forget Ms. Carson's contributions to this very successful project. Perhaps our new Service Desk Manager can make this his first tasking...Jackson, I believe you have a few announcements of your own?" Mr. Ferguson said, paving the way for Jackson Jones to speak next.

"Although it was Tabitha's vision; had it not been for Justin Smith and Rudy Vargas, this project would not have been completed. I can think of no other person more qualified to be the first Service Desk Manager than Rudy…come on over here please." Jackson said.

Rudy walked over to Jackson, stunned at what he'd just heard. Jackson extended his hand in congratulations as did Mr. Ferguson.

"Without Rudy's dedication to the Service Desk concept, none of us would be standing here today…Outstanding job and congratulations on your promotion." Jackson continued, shaking Rudy's hand again.

A smattering of applause rose up again. When the applause subsided, Jackson continued.

"Additionally, as some of you know Steve Parker is retiring as the DSS Lead and we will have an appropriate ceremony to celebrate his years of faithful service to the company…But at this time I would like to officially name his replacement. Justin step forward please." Jackson implored. Justin stepped forward; just as shocked by the announcement as Rudy had been moments earlier.

"Months ago, I had an opportunity to speak with Justin and I asked him if he thought IT Service Management had a place within our IT department. That was the beginning of this journey in which Justin sought out advice and information and ultimately came up with the Service Desk recommendation, which we approved. Along the way he drafted Rudy to join in the journey. So what you see before you is the result of a simple question posed to one employee. Resulting in better services provided to every employee and customer from this day forward. Justin, I can think of no one better suited or qualified to take over the DSS team lead, congratulations." Jackson said as the applause began again.

Justin and Rudy stood in front of the crowd, pleased but uncomfortable in the limelight. Sensing this, Jackson spoke up.

"Somebody start cutting the cake! Time to celebrate!"

"Did we just get promoted to supervisory positions?" Rudy leaned over to his friend and asked in a hushed tone while everyone else beat a path to the cake.

"I think so." Justin responded standing in shocked

bewilderment. "Now you and Samm really have something to celebrate!"

"I guess so. And you, the DSS Lead? That's pretty awesome." Rudy said.

"Boys, what are you doing standing over here by yourselves? Come join the celebration." Jackson said as he walked over to where the boys were standing.

"I think we're just surprised." Rudy said.

"You mean shocked." Justin corrected.

"Why? You both certainly deserve the promotions…not to mention the jobs come with nice salary adjustments, if you know what I mean. You're management now boys." Jackson said with a smile and a wink. "Come on, let's get you some cake."

Jackson wrapped his left arm around Rudy's shoulder and his right around Justin's shoulder and led them both toward the celebration and into their new futures as company management.

Conclusion

As you may recall from "Justin and Rudy's Excellent IT Adventure," this story began with a question posed by the company CIO to a single employee (Justin). The question was, "Is IT Service Management worth our time and effort for our company?" From that simple and rather innocuous question rose a new way of doing business within the IT department of the Southern United Insurance Company. For a company to find better ways of doing business; it must begin with simple and basic questions and someone or a team must provide answers the company leadership can act upon.

I think most would agree that Justin and Rudy were untapped assets within the company. When asked to rise to the challenge they certainly did; even when challenges and tragedies were thrown in their paths. Both clearly illustrated what can be accomplished when there is a drive to be successful and improve the working conditions within the workplace. For their efforts, they were ultimately recognized as company leaders and promoted.

On to a few other notes...Jackson Jones didn't have much of a bright future as the CIO; in fact, it's safe to say he was on shaky ground and in over his head from the start. What turned things around for him? A few things really, but putting his trust in Justin and Rudy to deliver what they promised went a long way in showing Jackson he had talented IT staff he could really count on. I would like to think Rudy and Samm will have a long life together and their relationship post-Service Desk project will flourish. But, since he just got promoted at the conclusion of our story; one never knows what further challenges he may encounter while establishing the Service Desk and the impact it may have on his relationship with Samm…let's hope it all works out.

    Regarding Justin, unfortunately, we will never know what kind of potential future he may have had with Tabitha. But we did get a glimpse into his resolve at being able to deal with her death and continuing to push the project along, in spite of his loss. Maybe his plan all along was to ensure a legacy for Tabitha. Or perhaps he did it as a coping mechanism to deal with her death. In truth, it was probably a little of both. The one thing we can conclude regarding Justin and Rudy is that; although at times tragic, it was certainly an ADVENTURE.

FEEL FREE TO POST COMMENTS ON MY AUTHOR'S PAGE:

amazon.com/author/michaelacton

www.ingramcontent.com/pod-product-compliance
Lightning Source LLC
Chambersburg PA
CBHW070242190526
45169CB00001B/266